IØ192103

After retiring in 1991 as a United Methodist pastor, Stanley C. Brown continued his avocation of research and writing regional history. For thirty years his family had a summer home on the upper East Verde River, which stimulated his fascination with the prehistoric and historic stories of the Rim Country. In 1993 he and his wife Ruth made their permanent home in Payson, and for twelve years he was appointed by the Town of Payson as its official historian. He served a number of years on the board of directors for the Northern Gila County Historical Society, including a time as its president, and developed the first historical archive for the Rim Country Museum. He has written weekly and bi-weekly columns for the *Payson Roundup* and has had numerous papers published in the *Journal of Arizona History*. His books and a historical novel are available at the museum. In 2004 the Browns moved to Arizona's first territorial capital, Prescott, where Stan continues his research and writing.

THEY WOULD NOT BE CONQUERED

A History of the
Tonto Apache Tribe

Stanley C. Brown

Copyright 2015 by Stanley C. Brown
Published 2015 by the Rim Country Press
P.O. Box 2532
Payson, AZ 85547
Tel: 928-474-3483
rimcountrymuseums.com

CONTENTS

Preface

PREFACE

In May of 1926 the director of the State Museum on the campus of the University of Arizona, Tucson, answered a letter of inquiry from a Mrs. Matthews in San Francisco about the Tonto Apaches. In his reply was this comment, "Regarding the Tonto Apaches, I fear I can be of very little help to you. I know of nothing that has been written upon this group. They are now mixed into the other groups in the White Mountain's Tribe at Fort Apache and at San Carlos. But I know of no one who has traced their history."

If I were to answer Mrs. Matthews I would have to give the same answer today. Much research has been done on the war waged by Euro-Americans against the Apaches and there have been numerous studies of prehistoric settlement in the territory later occupied by the Tonto Apache. But no one has gathered the available information and provided us with a written history of the small tribe called Tonto Apache.

The reason so little has been written about this fascinating subject can be readily understood. When the European culture began its migration westward across America, Arizona was essentially a bridge to California gold. As the Pacific connection grew, so did the necessity for better trails to connect the vast stretches of the continent. As trails became roads and then railroads, they followed routes along the Gila River in the south and across the Colorado Plateau in the north. In either case, they skirted the wilderness of central Arizona and left out the territory of the Tonto Apache. The terrain, with its rugged canyons, ridges and mountains, lay in a northwest by southeast direction and created an impossible barrier for east-west travel. The Apaches who lived in these basins and mountains were, therefore, the last Arizona natives to be threatened by the settlement of those they called "White-eyes." This moniker originated because the white of Caucasian eyeballs contrasts with the coffee color of Indian eyeballs. As for the Apache people, they refer to themselves as "The People." In their language it is Nde, pronounced En-dah, and implies a people set apart and superior to other peoples.

When the California gold rush was over and miners began to prospect in the central mountains of Arizona, word got out about the lush grazing lands and the abundance of game waiting to be exploited by ranchers and miners and those who serviced them. Once these Americans settled in Arizona they began to encroach on Tonto Apache lands. Settlers became prime targets for Apaches and the various Pai groups who stole livestock for food. This created the need for a military presence to protect the settlers and it was the beginning of the end for the old way of life among the Tontos. As we shall see, however, they are "The People Who Would Not Be Conquered." Their story deserves to be told and honor given to their history.

As I attempt to put together the exciting and dramatic story of these people who live in the Rim Country and Verde River Valley, credit must go to many who have helped me over the years. Alan Ferg, Nicolas P. Hauser, Keith Basso, George S. Esper, and Thomas Hinton are among those to whom I am deeply indebted. Also of great help were the archives of the Arizona Historical Society of Tucson, the Sharlot Hall Museum Library in Prescott; the Fort Verde State Park Museum in Camp Verde; the Cline Library at Northern Arizona University,

Flagstaff; the Colter Library of the Northern Arizona Museum, Flagstaff; The Hayden Library, Special Collections, at Arizona State University, Tempe, and the Arizona Historical Foundation in that same location; The Department of Library Archives and Public Records at the state capitol in Phoenix; The Smithsonian Institution in Washington and the National Archives and Records Administration in Washington, D.C. and in Laguna Niguel, California.

In the Payson area, journalist Carroll Cox did much over the years to gather information about the Tonto Apaches and publish it from her several journalistic positions. She deserves much credit for being the first person to systematically write a simple history of the Tonto Apaches and publish it in a 1987 series in *The Mogollon Advisor*.

I hope the reader will be inspired and enlightened by this story and that young Tonto Apaches will be encouraged to embrace the heritage they have all but lost. If I were a Tonto Apache and could speak in the tongue of the ancestors, I could better tell the odyssey, the joy, the struggle, and the terror of their story. However, I am White-eyes, and I write as White-eyes. All I can do is ask forgiveness from the people I have come to appreciate so heartily.

Stanley C. Brown

Chapter 1

THE TONTOS' OWN STORY OF BEGINNINGS

The bronzed index finger of the youthful student was over a topographic map of Arizona, seeking the exact geographical center. Then, with the guidance of his grandfather, the lad's finger slowly descended and came to rest.

"You are in the heart of your homeland," said the aging man. "Here the Din-eh lived and died, and live

"The Din-eh?" quizzed the youth.

"That is the name we call ourselves. You have only heard the name Tonto. The white-eyes gave us that name. Some Indian tribes call us Apache, which in their language meant the *enemy*."

The youth and his grandfather sat together in the shade of a Utah juniper, the map propped on their knees as they leaned against the tree trunk. Around them on the hillside were the modern houses of the small Tonto Apache Reservation in Payson, Arizona, staring like occupants in an amphitheater. The Apache youth could hear activity from the nearby Mazatzal Casino, set beside State Route 87, where a representative headdress of a Spirit Dancer caps the casino entrance. This was a constant reminder of Usen's presence, the Apache name for God.

The boy's grandfather hoped to create in the young Apache an interest in their tribal past. Not many of the younger generation seemed to care, taken up with public school activities, sports, and pressured by the Euro-American culture. They had not learned to speak the language and with the elimination of the language the past was rapidly being lost. Although the genocide of Apaches failed as the goal of 19th century Americans, the elimination of their culture was almost complete by the end of the 20th century. The grandfather knew how important it was to recover the honorable history of the Tonto Apaches, as well as that of the western Yavapai. Families from the two tribes had intermarried over many years.

"This is our land, my son," said the grandfather as his extended arm swept in a broad ellipse. "Our people have lived from the top of the Mazatzal Mountains on the southwest, to the Verde River on the west, across the uplands of the Mogollon Rim on the north, throughout the Sierra Ancha range on the east, and south to the Salt River."

"Is the Rim what our people call Black Mesa?" interrupted the lad.

"Yes. The Invaders named that whole plateau, and the mountains east of here, after a Spanish governor of New Mexico, Juan Ignacio Flores Mogollon."

The lad stared for a few moments at the map, considering the landmarks his grandfather had designated. "What does his name mean?"

"My son, I don't know. Our Apache names all have important meanings, but I do not know if the white-eyes have names with meaning."

The boy continued his questioning. "What does Mazatzal mean?"

His grandfather could answer that one. "Your cousins, the Yavapai, who lived on the west side of the mountains, called them Maz-at-zark, and held up four fingers for the Four Peaks. Do you remember the Apache word I taught you for mountain?"

"Dzil," replied the boy after touching his forehead with the palm of his hand for memory.

"Some of the white people I have talked to say the name comes from the Aztec language and Mazatzal means `the place of the deer.' But our people called that range `Rocks In a Line Of Greenness.' The name comes from a band of our people who lived on the east side of the mountains. They were called 'Rocks In a Line of Greenness People.'"

The boy's lips moved as he attempted to pronounce the names in Apache. "Our people were here a very long time, weren't they grandfather? Tell me the story again of how we got here."

"Long ago they say..."

The boy quickly responded, "Ya!" as he had been taught whenever a story was begun in this way. Then grandfather could continue.

"Long ago, after the Gaan made earth and sky, there were no people living on the earth. Underneath there were places where the Red Ants were living, and they were talking about this country up here. The Red Ant chief talked about coming up here, and all the ants decided, `Alright, let's go up to this new place.'

"There was a big, tall agave stem growing there, up and up to the sky. The Red Ant People began to climb this stalk, and each time they came to a joint they made camp for the night. Up and up they went, until finally the chief told them to look around at this place where they were. There were lots of good foods growing, and the chief told them to bring those foods into their camp. The people went all over the country for these wild foods, and there was lots to eat. They brought them back, and then they went out again to gather more of the good foods. The chief would sing a song, and every time he sang the song the people would come together again. Finally the chief said, `This is your land. Go anywhere you want, and when the place is good stop there and settle.

"So this is the place they lived, and those first people were our ancestors, the Red Ants."

The young anthropologist, Grenville Goodwin, was the first to study the Western Apaches and this story is based on what he heard from them. In the stories of Tonto Apaches, The Place of Emergence was considered to be north of their historic territory. As we shall see, this is close to modern scientific understanding.

Chapter Two

APACHE ORIGINS

Tonto Apache people are told in the stories of their fathers that they emerged as a people not far to the north from where they now live. The more scientific story of Apache beginnings is not a few miles to the north, but many thousands of miles to the north and many thousands of years ago. It is a story that so far has no traceable beginnings, so we shall dip in at the close of the Pleistocene period during the Ice Age. The repeated advance of glaciers from the north had depleted Earth's oceans. One of these glacial advances, called the Wisconsin Ice Age, advanced into North America fifty thousand years ago and reached its peak about twenty five thousand years later. During this time period the oceans of the world were lowered about 300 feet and a land bridge between Asia and North America appeared in the present location of the Bering Strait. That Ice Age lasted until 11,000 years ago though we should not imagine the land bridge was available throughout the entire period. It was more like a drawbridge, which was down from fifteen to twenty four thousand years ago and down again from about nine to eleven thousand years ago. Nor was it a matter of jumping from stone to stone across the puddle. This bridge was big, a strip of dry land perhaps 1,200 miles wide! It enabled people from the continent of Asia to migrate from Siberia to Alaska.

Once human beings had mastered fire and clothing and techniques of survival they were ready to follow the mastodons, mammoths, and bison on which they subsisted. There were several migrations of these hunter-gatherers and each became trapped on the new continent by a rising sea. Those who arrived in North America 15,000 years ago were probably not the first to come. Recent discoveries suggest the possibility of an occupation much earlier than that, even suggesting a European presence here first.

We do know that ice masses converged in Canada to block a further southward migration. They later parted near the close of the age. This presented an open door for migration on the east side of the Rocky Mountains. We also know that by 11,300 years ago the mammoth hunters had reached Arizona, wielding projectile points and atlatls strong enough to kill their prey. These were the Clovis people, named for the place in New Mexico where their spear points were first identified. At least one of these spear points has been found in the Rim Country. When the prehistoric animals they followed died out the people also seem to disappear. Perhaps they migrated elsewhere, or over the centuries learned to adapt their culture to changing environments and emerged as those we call The Ancient Ones, or Ancestral Puebloans.

More to our interest is the fact that while the Clovis people were hunting in Arizona, about 10,000 years ago, another wave of migrants was crossing the drawbridge into Alaska and Canada. They would be the Athapaskans and because the "native people" of northwest Canada and Alaska today are mostly Athapaskan in their genetic makeup, language and culture, we assume they were among these more recent arrivals from Asia.

The origin of the name "Athapaskan" is from a Cree Indian word meaning the "place where there is grass everywhere." That place is just west of Lake Athabaska in extreme northwestern Alberta, Canada. It was adopted as the family name of the people who lived there. The word can be spelled either *Athabaskan* or *Athapaskin*.

As the glaciers of the Pleistocene era receded Athapaskan bands migrated east and south following the animals and plants. By 5,000 B.C. they had reached Washington State, adapting to the changing ecology as they went. Then sometime from A.D. 1,000 to 1,500, a large group of Athapaskans broke away from the others and began a southward migration along the eastern edge of the Rocky Mountains. While the exact route of their migration is a subject of debate among anthropologists and archaeologists, the theory generally accepted is this: as the Athapaskans spread south some of their groups became the plains people called Kiowa and Comanche. They were hunting buffalo on the Great Plains about A.D. 1300.

Another grouping of Athapaskans moved along the edges of the Rocky Mountains and entered the Southwest from the north about A.D. 1400. These would become the Navajo and Western Apache, developing a markedly different lifestyle than the plains Indians. They learned their lifestyle in part from the pueblo dwellers they encountered and with whom they traded meat and hides for pottery and seed. At times they would raid these same communities for goods and food. Thus they came to be thought of as "the enemy," the English translation of a Zuni word.

Chapter Three

SETTLING A HOMELAND

In their new surroundings of central Arizona and New Mexico, it was necessary for the Apaches to learn how to subsist in the dry, desert climate. They needed to know the kinds of game to hunt, the fruits and their seasons, and the places where all of these were to be found. They encountered a culture that had preceded them from which they could learn and borrow. We have called these earlier people by many names: Anasazi, Mogollon, Hohokam, Sinagua, and Salado. Those in the Payson area have been identified as perhaps even older, a different race nicknamed "Bunheads" because of the large occipital extension on the back of their skulls. All of these "ancient people" reached a high point of development around A.D. 1350 after which they seemed to disappear. Apparently they became so numerous throughout the southwest that, according to scholars, it was overpopulation coupled with a severe drought that caused their demise. Possibly pressure from the invading Athapaskans added to their retreat. In any case, their successors are supposedly found among the pueblo dwellers of Arizona and New Mexico. Such conclusions continue to be a matter of discussion among anthropologists.

Meanwhile, the Athapaskan migrants were becoming "Apaches," enemies who were not exactly welcomed. They branched into distinctive groups: the Navajo in the Four Corners region, the Jicarilla and Mescalero in New Mexico, the Chiricahua in southeastern Arizona, northern Sonora and Chihuahua, and the Western Apache in central Arizona. This latter group ranged from Flagstaff on the north to Tucson on the south, from the Verde River on the west to Springerville on the east. It was a vast area and according to Grenville Goodwin, the first white man to study them, these people divided into five distinct groupings, each with family bands and semi-bands. The five groups are White Mountain, Cibecue, San Carlos, Northern Tonto, and Southern Tonto.

The Northern and Southern Tonto Apaches occupied a quiet land, shattered only by the call of elk in rut or the scream of a lion asserting its authority. Lightning from the summer monsoon would split the air, shattering trees and igniting the fires that brought new life to the forest. After the long drought that pushed the fragile lifeline over the edge for the ancient ones, summer and winter rains had returned. The land waited for new occupants to rediscover its multiple riches.

It remains for archaeologists and anthropologists to determine the decade or even the century the people we call Tonto took up residence in the basins and mountains of The Rim Country. It is certain that another group, the Yavapai, were coming in from the west about this same time, perhaps arriving slightly before the Apaches who entered from the east and north. The intermingling of these two groups was inevitable. Their lifeways were so similar that experts are unable to distinguish between their artifacts and campsites.

It was during the 16th century, while the Tontos and Yavapai were taking possession of central Arizona, the Spanish Conquistadores explored northward from Mexico. There are no records of the Spanish entering directly into the Tonto territory, though they came close when visiting the Zuni, the Hopi, and entering the Verde River Valley. The Rim Country appears on European and Spanish maps as Tierra Incognita, the unknown land. It was such a rugged and isolated place the Spaniards avoided it. They apparently decided any precious metals that might be there were not recoverable. When travel between New Mexico and California later became important, the Apache country was not only dangerous but out of the way. It was far better to use routes south or north of the central mountains. Thus the Tonto Apaches and Yavapai could mingle and develop their own way of life for 250 years without interference from an encroaching world of white-eyes.

Grenville Goodwin relates a story told by an Apache named *Old Man He Goes To War*. It told of a time when the Apache had not yet moved into the Tonto Basin but had come only as far west as Cibecue and San Carlos. When some of them explored the Tonto Basin they encountered what they called the "sand house people." They made friends with these cliff dwellers and some of the Apaches moved close to them. But trouble erupted when the cliff dwellers accused the Apaches of thievery and war ensued. The ancient people abandoned their houses and moved down into the Salt River Valley.

Such stories indicate that not all of the Ancient Puebloans had disappeared before the Tonto Apaches entered the area. It is probably safe to say the people who became Tontos settled in the Payson environs around 1600. Some scholars believe the Yavapai arrived 100 years before that. Frequented campsites for these two groups included Rye Creek and Gisela, Indian Gardens and Christopher Creek, as well as the uplands of Payson and Pine.

Chapter Four

THE YAVAPAI CONNECTION

As the Tonto Apache bands settled into their new environment, they began to develop small plots of agriculture and established camps in the valleys near the creeks. They returned seasonally to their upland camps where they could exploit resources such as wild game, chert for arrow and spear points, agave, pine nuts, acorns and a host of other plants and berries.

The legends of the Tonto Apaches tell that the Mountain Spirits, or Gaan, built some of the prehistoric ruins and caves and left their artifacts for the Apaches to use. Numerous petroglyphs were thought to be messages left by the Mountain Spirits when they retreated in disgust over the disobedience of The People to their teaching. The Apaches felt a strong spiritual link with the ancient ones whom they followed and prehistoric sites were considered sacred. Tonto Apaches would go to the sacred caves and springs to seek a blessing on their hunts, offering baskets, colored stones, petrified wood and prayer feathers.

From the time of their entrance into the Rim Country, the Tontos met and mingled with another people, the Yuman-speaking Yavapai. It is reported how two Yavapai Indians at Fort McDowell were conversing in the 1970s. "I don't know about the white people. I do not know who they are or where they come from. But we people don't come from nowhere across the ocean. We were raised here in this country. We come out at Sedona, the middle of the world. This is our home."

They were reflecting the oral tradition of their people, that long ago all living beings ascended into this world through a place called *Ahagaskiaywa*, "place where the people came out first." Today it is called Montezuma's Well near Camp Verde in Arizona's Verde Valley. Those who continued to live in the Sedona area called themselves **Wipukpa** (or Wipukpaya). The tradition goes on to say the other groups of Yavapai people spread from there.

Anthropologists might wish their ideas of Yavapai origin could be that simple. Instead, the discussion revolves around several theories. Most likely the Yavapai are a Yuman speaking people who migrated from California after A.D. 1100. This would seem to be affirmed by their Pai dialect with its Yuman roots. In addition to the Yavapai ("people of the mountains"), others of this lineage include the Hualapai ("people of the red earth") and the Havasupai ("people of the blue-green water").

In their diaspora the Yavapai formed several sub-tribes. For the Americans, to whom all Indians looked alike, they were all simply Apaches or Mojave-Apaches. In the decades of American-Apache warfare the Yavapai name faded into disuse while every pillage by the Yavapai was attributed to Apaches. Furthermore, since the Tontos were notorious the epithet "Tonto Apache" was even associated with raids that occurred far from Tonto territory.

The confusion in calling Yavapai by the name Apache does not sit well with the Yavapai people, who rightly feel it cheats them out of a unique heritage. Even today the Yavapai use indigenous names for their several groups. "The Quivkopaya are here," say those in the Verde Valley when their relatives from Ft. McDowell come to visit. It means "the elsewhere people." The Quivkopaya territory went along the west side of the Mazatzal Mountains, throughout the Superstition Mountains, and east along the Salt River to today's Hayden, Arizona. Their raids reached as far south as the Catalina Mountains and Tucson. Today their descendents can be found living on the Fort McDowell Yavapai Reservation.

The group named Yavapaya lived in the upper Verde Valley around Jerome and Mingus Mountain and all around the Prescott area. Their descendants can be found on the Yavapai Reservation in and around Camp Verde. A third group, the Tulkepaya, was west of the Prescott area, and once subdued by the U.S. Army they were settled on a reservation at Date Camp. During the years of the Rio Verde Reservation (1871-1875) Yavapai and Tonto Apaches surrendered in order to save their lives and were made to live together. Then in 1875 all the Yavapai groups were force-marched along with the Tontos to the San Carlos Reservation on the Gila River. There they languished until they were allowed to drift back to their homelands. Only in modern times were they able to establish their right to sovereignty on their own reservations.

One observant soldier stationed at the Rio Verde Reservation, Sergeant Robert H. Walker, made a comparison of the differences between the Apache and Yavapai. He pointed out that they were two distinct peoples, something most whites had been slow to understand. The Yavapai were taller, of muscular build and thickly featured. The Tonto Apaches were slight and less muscular, smaller in stature and finely featured. While the Yavapai were often tattooed, the Apache seldom showed any such decoration.

Chapter Five

APACHE LIFE WAYS

The life styles of the Tonto Apache and Yavapai people were so similar anthropologists and archeologists found it almost impossible to distinguish between the campsites and villages they left behind. They were both hunter-gatherers and they mingled, even intermarried, from the early decades of their mutual arrival in the Rim Country. They often used the same campsites alternately or simultaneously.

The most definitive indication that the Tonto Apache and Yavapai are two distinct people is in their respective languages. John Bourke, crisscrossing the area as General George Crook's aide in the campaigns of 1871-74, recognized immediately that they were dealing with separate tribes. The Western Apache of the Tonto Basin and Mogollon Rim, Bourke reported, were not pure Apache like those of the White Mountains, but had intermixed with the Yuman speaking group. Most of them spoke both languages, he said, and the head men had two names, one each from both traditions.

Other reported observations made it clear these were two different peoples. The Yavapai had long hair in the back but cut at the ears, and it was coal black. The Tontos wore their hair cut short at the shoulders and squared off in front just above the eyes. Its color was not black so much as a yellowish-brown or auburn tint.

A significant study was made in 1965 by David M. Brugge, tracing names used in the two languages as they are spoken today among various Indian communities of Central Arizona. Tracing the frequency of Yuman and Athapaskan rooted names used by persons born in different locations, he determined on a community by community basis the amount of mixing that had taken place. The study confirmed that there were two different tribes who mixed and subsequently created a unique grouping of people. Individuals and families often claimed to be pure Apache or pure Yavapai, but for the most part, they admitted to carrying the genes from both sides.

Over generations of close contact in central Arizona, the Yavapai adopted Apache clan systems and their material culture became identical to the Tonto Apache. Even Apache myths of creation strongly influenced those of the Yavapai. It is also true that the Yavapai influenced the Tontos. Dr. Brugge notes the Tonto Apaches have a dialect different from other Western Apaches. There is a slight "Yavapai accent" in the speech of the Tontos. It is this rather "sing-song" dialect among Tontos that caused the White Mountain, Pinal, Cibecue and other Apache groups to call them "foolish," or in Spanish, "Tonto."

In recent years it has become "politically incorrect" for Tontos or Yavapai people to admit to all of this mingling. Each group is jealous of their separate heritage. As I interviewed tribal elder Vince Randall, living in the Middle Verde Valley, he traced his lineage on both his mother's and father's sides to pureblooded Tonto Apache. He stated that his mother belonged to the *Over-The-Rim* band, which ranged all the way from Heber and Snowflake to Ashfork. I asked him, "Does that mean your mother was what the anthropologists call `Northern Tonto'?"

He answered smiling, "That is a misnomer. I always say (those anthropologists) put in the Mason-Dixon line. There really is no Northern-Southern (difference). It's all N'de, all the way down to the Salt and Verde Rivers... Of course they were roaming all of the country. We are all inter-related."

Each of the family units, or bands, would oversee a specific hunting and farming territory. A Tonto Apache knew his well-defined hunting ground like the back of his hand. Every place had a name and every name contained a story. Within his own area he felt the power of each place and there he was master of the hunt. These place-name stories were vital to him because they told how to live the good life and how to subsist in this location. The older members of the family had given them to him from the time he was a child. He would pass them on to his children's children. If he transgressed into the hunting ground of another band he lost his power and felt helpless.

This was not his land; these were not his stories. If he did not know the stories or the place names in another band's territory, how could he know where the elk ran or where the berries grew? He could lose his way.

However, not all the seasonal produce could be counted on unless a family did venture outside their traditional boundaries. This required permission of the neighboring band. These frequent migrations added to the genetic mix among Yavapai and Apache. Friendly trade and intermarriage between the bands led to alliances and they would come together when necessary to vigorously defend the entire territory against intrusion from other cultures, white or Indian.

Chapter Six

THE STORIES OF PLACES

Hiking down the headwaters of the East Verde River I feel embraced by the solitude. As the canyon deepens, the arms of the Mogollon Rim reach around in a motherly embrace. The ponderosa pine forest endows my head with its sweet scents of perfume and vanilla. The soft swish of wind through the boughs whispers words of praise and joy. Springs, set free from the hillsides splash into the waters of the river and delight my ears with their music. My eyes gladden at the sparkle of dancing water as it runs in rivulets and dives over rocks.

Suddenly, a snap in the undergrowth startles me! I stop to listen. It is the presence of Apaches. They are here! I know it! This is their land; this is where they harvested the pinon, acorn, and raspberry. This is where they hid when white soldiers invaded their land. This is where every jutting landmark, every stream and ridge, every stand of trees, every streamside field is endowed with a story. Each is gathered up in a descriptive Apache name and has a lesson to teach about what it means to be The N'de.

The spirits of native people are watching me here, because I am the invader. I have come to love this land and use it for my own purposes, but my roots are not as deep as are theirs. I have no real idea of what this land means to them, about its sacredness and how inseparable they are from it. If we who are not Apache are to learn their story and appreciate their culture, we will have to settle for a non-Indian kind of history. Apache history is oral and living, shared in the community and never by the isolated act of reading a book. Apache history is carried in stories, and when they are told, they bring the past into the present. The storyteller with grand imagination gives speech to the mysterious presence of the ancestors.

Apache history has no interest in dates or a sequence of events so important to my European thought process. For them linear time bends into a circle, and the past is now; the place is everything. Anthropologist Keith Basso explains this clearly in his book *Wisdom Sits in Places* (University of New Mexico Press, Albuquerque, 1996). When the Apache tell a story, the listener enters a world where fact is not as important as truth. Truth is measured by morality and is embodied in the story. Taken together the Apache stories, like the Christian's Bible, chart the way of the good life. The lessons they teach are tied not to time but to places and the events of those places. The concise and highly sophisticated language of the Apache embodies the story in the place-name. To live in the land is to encounter the places. Those places in turn remind an Apache of how to live, the way that works best, the way given by the ancestors.

For example, Keith Basso tells of a Cibecue Apache girl who attended a sacred ceremony with her hair rolled up in pink plastic curlers. He was present to observe the whispers of disdain from her elders, though no one spoke directly to the girl. She had just come home from boarding school and was probably feeling her independence. The ceremony was the Sunrise Dance, a girl's puberty celebration where the women of all ages are expected to wear their hair free flowing. Such respect for the accepted customs is vital to the effectiveness of the ceremony. Here the honored girl receives the qualities of character that she will carry as an adult.

A few weeks later, the student who had broken the revered custom at the puberty ceremony had returned again to the reservation to celebrate a cousin's birthday at the camp of their maternal grandmother. Basso was again present and observed the significant way the pink-curler girl now received her chastisement. After the meal her grandmother began to tell a story. At a place called *Men-Stand-Above-Here-And-There*, one of the Apache police arrested a fellow for killing a white man's cow. While the policeman was taking the fugitive to an army officer at Fort Apache, his mind became confused. On two different attempts he was unable to verbalize a charge against the man he had arrested. Instead, he made meaningless talk with the army officer. "Something was working with the words in his mind," said the grandmother. Unable to press charges, the policeman took the man back to the place called *Men-Stand-Above-Here-and-There*, and released him.

When the grandmother finished retelling this story, the rebellious girl rose and left the family circle and returned home without a word. Two years later Keith Basso happened to be talking with this same young woman and they recalled the previous incident. She admitted that her grandmother had, as they say, shot an arrow at her with that story. She perceived in the story that the policeman had gone against Apache customs in denying one of his own people food. It would have been a good thing for the hunter to feed his family with the white man's cow. The policeman had become subject to some kind of witchcraft which confused his mind because he sided with the white man's law instead of Apache morality. The girl knew in her heart that it would be so with others, who like herself went against the customs of the people.

Upon going home in tears that night she had thrown those pink curlers away, and ever since then the place in the story, *Men-Stand-Above-Here-and-There*, haunted her whenever she passed by. The place and its story-charged name became a continuous reminder to her of the good way an Apache was to live.

Chapter Seven

APACHE BANDS AND CLANS

The central mountains of Arizona offered a wide variety of climates and the Tontos migrated to warmer lowlands in winter and cooler uplands in summer. Gathering parties would go out from base camps, or *rancherias*, to follow the procession of the harvest. This often required entering the territory of a neighboring band but as long as there was an abundance of food such intrusions were acceptable. In the spring there were the hearts of agave to be roasted in fire-pits. In early summer there were cactus fruits and mesquite beans; in late summer the corn and squash were ready along the streams; in the fall pinion nuts and acorns were harvested. All this kept the people on the move.

Socializing at common gathering places was a welcome time of exchange. A period of drought would send the Tontos toward the Salt and Black Rivers to mingle with other Western Apache groups, or west to the Verde River for more mixing with the Yavapai. Times of drought thus became a signal for greater migrations and genetic exchanges. Each band was subdivided into local family groups and each local group had a chief, or headman, chosen by mutual agreement. He directed the cooperative activities of raiding, food gathering and dealing with other bands. Each local group was composed of two to six family clusters and, together as an extended family, they formed an effective cooperative with a division of labor. The men would hunt, raid, fight wars and do the heaviest work. The women would care for the livestock, prepare the food, care for the children, and make the household implements. They also gathered the wild foods and did most of the agricultural work, as well as build the family house, called a *gowa*. The word is adopted from a Yavapai word *gwa-bun*-yav, that literally means "family." The dwelling was 10 to 12 feet in diameter and looked like an inverted cone. The framework was made of slender poles stuck into the ground in a circle, bent together and tied at the top. Branches, bear grass or hides were spread over this frame. There was a vent at the top for the fire smoke. The floor was dug down several inches and the dirt piled around the perimeter inside and out. A common word for these dwellings is *wickiup*, but that term was brought west by the white man who heard it from Sac and Fox Indians.

The children of the local group all related as brothers and sisters, though most of them were cousins. Each Apache belonged to his or her mother's clan, tracing his or her relationship through a maternal line of ancestors. That line would go back to someone who had established a farm at the clan's legendary place of origin. In the matrilineal social structure of the Tontos, the husband would go to live with his wife's family. A matrilineal social organization designates the line of descent and kinship through the mother instead of the father. Because one's clan was officially that of his or her mother, a Tonto Apache could have clan-kin among other Apache tribes. Clan members had mutual responsibility for each other and were obligated to come on summons to help defend or avenge one another. This meant that when necessary assistance could be drawn from beyond one's own band. Everyone also knew they were liable to suffer revenge from another clan for the misdeeds by one of their own members. Thus an individual was always conscious that his or her safety and survival rested on being a loyal part of the clan and he or she would carefully weigh actions which might bring revenge from other groups.

The primary deterrent from attack by others was to have a record of strong defense. If a clan was known for defending its rights and never tolerating the slightest infraction, then the chances were good that others would leave it alone. To be violent in response to infringements on the rights of a clan member was a key to survival. The only possible reason a person or clan would not defend their rights would be looked upon as weakness. Apaches neither considered nor understood the concept of love for enemies and forgiveness. Weakness or the appearance of weakness was a stigma to be avoided at all costs. Since survival was always marginal for hunter-gatherers, life was lived by Nature's law of survival of the fittest. It followed that the temptation was strong to violate any group that appeared to be weak. They were easy prey, not worthy of living in this wilderness setting, and one could feel justified in eliminating them.

Not only did clan membership lend strength to the family group, but also it enabled one to travel in the territories of other bands, accepting safe passage, food and lodging because of kinship in a given clan. Common facial features, mannerisms and dress were subtle proofs of clan membership. A special width or tilt to a head band could be the identifying mark. More obvious clan signs came in drawings of the clan's sacred animal or other symbols painted on the body, clothing or utilitarian vessels.

The clan also served to regulate marriage and prevent inbreeding. No one could marry a member of their mother's clan or one of several related clans, though it was permissible to marry someone of their father's clan.

Chapter Eight

THE RELIGION OF THE TONTO APACHE

Tonto Apaches all belong to a clan and each clan claims a distinct geographical area as its ancestral home. Over the generations clan members spread out from those areas, but somewhere in the soul of each there is a claim upon that place as "home." The collective name for the area around Payson is T-ehgo-tsudn, called "*the place of the yellow land*," referring to the crumbling yellow granite. These families call themselves the T'e'-'go'-tsuk" clan, "*People of the yellow speckled water*."

Other Tonto clan locations in the Rim Country include the Sierra Ancha near Young and Roosevelt called "*the place where cedars come out to a point*," or the Gat-chea-teen clan. West of Payson, along the East Verde River, is the origin of the No-go-zukn, "*line scratched in the earth*" or "*people of the crooked waters*." The clan from lower Tonto Creek near Gisela is from the Si'e-de-gi-'een', or "*A very sandy place*."

Lands, bands and clans were basic to the Tonto Apache's way of life, but so was religion. In 1871, one of the soldiers posted at the Rio Verde Reservation, a Sergeant Walker whose scrapbook is in the Sharlot Hall Museum, Prescott, made a comment about the Tontos that is frequently reflected in the writings of 19th and early 20th century historians. "These people have absolutely no religion. They believe neither in God nor in the Devil. They say that these ideas come from white men and are not true." However, he went on to describe their symbolic accoutrements, such as the prayer sticks and painted crosses used by medicine men. The symbol of the cross was confusing to white men who did not realize it represents the four sacred directions and that each quadrant represents a heaven or hereafter-place. A cross with a red circle around it represents the Giver of Life and the sunlight that is God's radiance and gift. These symbols and names for holy spirits were just too much for the white man to comprehend, enmeshed as he was in his own symbolism. "I regard these," said Walker, "rather as toys than as symbols of faith. I do not think that they (the Apache-Yavapai) believe anything."

The fact is Apache religion gave rise to lofty virtues such as chastity, speaking the truth, courage and loyalty. It was with almost complete ignorance of Apache culture that European-Americans questioned the faith of the N'de, "The People." Yet the Apaches believed their ancestors had climbed up from the underworld on an agave stalk with as much certainty as Christians believed in the historical Jesus or the Genesis story of Creation. "God" in Apache is Ussen (variously spelled in English Yusn or Usen), The Life Giver. He created the universe and Changing Woman (the mother of the race), as well as her sons (Child Born of Water and Killer of Enemies). These two brothers prepared the Earth for N'de by killing many monsters.

It is true that the English word "religion" has no Apache equivalent. What white men did not understand is that faith in the supernatural is inseparable from the Apache's daily life. Every animate and inanimate object in nature is endowed with a living spirit and that spirit is treated with respect just as one treats another human being with respect. The source of all life, including the spirits, is the one God, Ussen, to whom one owes thanksgiving for everything, and to whom one directs daily prayers. Of course, Apache worship forms differ from those of European culture, so whites did not always recognize devotion when they saw it. Apache prayers are in the form of songs and chants, dances and symbolic acts, rising smoke and lived virtues. All of life is a prayer to Ussen, thus religion is not something set apart from the common things of every day, as it tends to be in European culture.

This pervasive spiritual outlook is embodied in the language and ceremonies of the Apache and is not something he would share with the white man. When invaders of his land questioned him on the significance of his acts of faith, or the sacred places he went to conduct rituals of prayer, the Apache was silent. Although a family band had no fixed place of residence in their wide-ranging territory, they did have fixed places known to be sacred. Devotion to these holy places and the spirits that inhabited them gave the Apache family its roots and often became seasonal places of residence. These holy places were known to be the dwellings of various Mountain

Spirits, or Men of the Mountain, called *Gaan*. They play for the Apache a similar role as angels, saints and the Holy Spirit in Christian belief. The Giver of Life knew how vulnerable human beings were in their struggle to live the good life, so he sent the *Gaan* as his representatives to teach them the right way. From them Apaches learned how to live the best way, how to hunt, heal their infirmities, how to plant and harvest, as well as how to discipline those who fall short of Ussen's design. Disgusted by human failure, the Gaan retreated to the other world and stationed themselves at the four cardinal points of the compass. However, in their benevolence, they still return through sacred caves in the mountains to teach, bless and chastise.

Chapter Nine

APACHE POWER

Our human need to see God manifested in some form is expressed when Apaches impersonate the Mountain Spirits, or *Gaan*, in special ceremonies. Masked dancers, secretly chosen, each create their own crown headdress, copying images left by the *Gaan* in petroglyphs. The dancer's personal identity is kept a mystery. The dancers do not literally become the Gaan during the dance ceremony, but they come close to it in the minds of the onlookers who make this identification. By the use of the dance and its mysterious participants, the power of the Mountain Spirits is present.

These Crown dancers play an especially important role in healing ceremonies, along with the Medicine Man or Shaman. Highly painted and decorated in the colors of the four directions, the dancers call out the evil spirits. One of the dancers is the clown and his task is to frighten away these evil spirits. After the dance, the heavy and awkward crowns are hidden away in a sacred cave, not to be disturbed.

One might recall the Christian belief that the Risen Christ is present in the elements of Holy Communion, or The Mass. Some groups hold that the bread and wine become in their essence the real presence of Christ's body and blood. Other groups believe the bread and wine are simply symbols of Christ's sacrifice on the cross. In that case, the mystery is that the resurrected Christ is among the worshippers as a living spiritual presence. This approaches the Apache's traditional belief regarding the crown dancers, whose presence calls upon the spiritual presence of the Gaan.

The Apache's understanding of his relationship to God is gathered up best in the concept of **power**. Power comes to a person in as many forms as there are human talents. It may be the power of being a swift runner, a leader among the people, an invincible warrior, a skillful hunter, or a healer. The list would have no end, but it is important to know that one does not go seeking after power and find it. Power is something that finds you and when you know you have it you are expected to use it for the good of the entire community. For example, during the puberty ceremony power is imparted to the young woman and when she becomes aware of her special gifts she will use them. Tribal members who exhibit one power or another will be looked to when circumstances call for that particular gift.

To understand his power, an Apache boy went off on what white men have called a "vision quest." After several days or a week of fasting in some high and hidden place, he communes with the *Gaan* and may be given his power. He does not return boasting about it, but keeps this as a very sacred part of his life. Whatever his power is, it will be manifest among his fellow Apaches. In time the tribe will look to him for the gifts he has demonstrated.

That person may develop a special ritual or ceremony designed to impart this gift to others, especially if it is the gift of healing. There are different medicines for different purposes, and the person in need may have to try a series of shamans, or "medicine men," before one of the ceremonies works for him or her.

I once encountered Apache "religion" in an unexpected event. It was June of 1990. My family and I had been evacuated from our home on the upper waters of the East Verde River during the Dude forest fire. Our home was spared by the effective work of the fire fighters and we were permitted to return as the fire lines were still being monitored. Each day a fire crew of Apaches would walk the line from the top of the Mogollon Rim down the East Verde River where they had stopped the fire. National Guard trucks would come to pick them up just a few hundred feet above our house and I talked with them as they concluded their day to head for the base camp on Houston Mesa.

One afternoon the supervisor of the crew donated his orders of the day to me. They included a poem written by one of the fire fighters. It was signed simply Goseyun, and entitled it **"A San Carlos Apache Wise One Clan Song**."

I immediately discovered that, to the Apache, this great, angry forest fire had become the symbol of prayer.

Climb a mountain,
    Gather Nature's wastes,
Build a fire,
    A huge angry fire;
Stretch Nature's skin
    And cover a hollow stump.
Beat the stretched skin
    To your heart's rhythm.
Chant a prayer
    And fill the valleys with echoes
    of your prayer.
Feel your spirit revive; yell out an angry
    scream to chase evil spirits away.
Be one in spirit with the Great Almighty
  One above.
The fire is there to show your spirit's revival.
A huge angry fire is a good sign.

Chapter Ten

WAR AND REVENGE

One reason the white-eyes did not understand the Apache's faith in God is because in American Christianity war and violence are thought of as evil. For the Apache, violence is part of life and does not conflict with their faith in the Life Giver and the Mountain Spirits.

The experience of James Kaywaykla, a Warm Springs Apache, is not unlike that of the Western Apache people. He was the narrator behind Eve Ball's book, *In The Days of Victorio*, (University of Arizona Press, Tucson, 1970) and he said, "Until I was about ten years old I did not know that people died except by violence... I had no doubt whatever but that I would die. I had never seen anything die a natural death, though I knew it happened. Everything died by violence and I wondered if I would suffer..."

Among the Tontos warfare was a deeply ingrained institution. There were rules to abide, there were ceremonies to perform before and after, there were prayers to be said and songs to be sung. War was not for winning territory but to prove courage and skill, to secure food, and to achieve revenge. To take the life of an enemy was not considered an evil act, but a cause to be celebrated and rewarded. To kill women and children was for them a blessing, because without their men to hunt and protect them they would be helpless and perhaps captured for slavery.

With the coming of the whites, the cruelty of Indian warfare intensified. Unscrupulous traders sold alcoholic beverages to the Indians, to which the Indian seemed especially vulnerable, and provided guns in trade. Mexican and American governments offered bounties for Indian scalps. This became a large business in the mid-19th century and if the black hair of a Mexican was long enough his scalp was often passed for an Apache. Traditionally it was not the practice of Apaches to take scalps, but when the invaders scalped Apaches, some were encouraged to return the favor and scalp their victims. However, when an Apache took a scalp it was after the victim was dead and then it was handled gingerly for fear of the dead person's ghost. The scalp was not brought back to camp, but carried for a day on a pole while prayers were offered for increased power. The victor might talk to the scalp, in effect praying that the group it represented would become weak. Only the Apaches' traditional enemies were scalped, like whites or Pimas or Mexicans.

The Apache did not have the elaborate governmental structures of the invaders. There were no legal systems, police forces, or standing armies. Apaches would organize themselves into war or raiding parties to protect their territory against others who would upset the delicate balance of their subsistence. At such times a war chief was chosen to lead them on their mission. If their numbers were not strong enough to assure victory, they would call upon other family groups in their same tribe and often reached beyond their territory to enlist fellow clan members who were obliged to respond. A Tonto Apache might have kin among the White River or Cibecue or Pinal people, who would, upon invitation, come to help defend or avenge their fellow clan members.

However, violent actions against other groups were weighed carefully since they would probably bring reciprocity. By the same token, if your band was known to have a strong fighting spirit and invincible defense, that could deter others from raiding your people. Keeping up a vicious front, whether you felt like it or not, was critical. Even the appearance of weakness was a stigma to be avoided; it was an invitation to annihilation.

Just as there was no Apache word for religion, so there was no word in the language for forgiveness. Once the need for revenge was established, it might come at any unsuspected moment in the future. Such a commitment lurked unrelenting in the thoughts and plans of the clan. The hour would be well chosen. When it came, the attack might seem far removed from the initial cause but those involved would know why and what for.

Tonto Apaches did not use the war club, which was a basic weapon of the Pima, Maricopa and Mohave tribes. When Tonto Apaches were accused of depredations using war clubs (as in the infamous Oatman Massacre), one is suspicious the raiders were really from desert tribes. The weapons of choice among Tonto Apaches were bows and arrows and lances made from the stalk of the agave or sotol (yucca plants). They were reinforced with rawhide and a bayonet blade of steel or sharp wood was attached to the end of the lance. The whole weapon measured anywhere from 4 to 15 feet in length. The lance was thrust directly into the victim, never thrown.

The Apaches were also excellent at making arrows. Their arrow was a 3 foot long shaft, the bow 5 feet high. Their skill brought deadly accuracy and the arrow point often carried poison made from rotting deer liver and snake venom.

Chapter Eleven

MARRIAGE AND THE FAMILY

The wardrobe of the Tonto Apache was basic and simple. Standard dress for the male began with a breechcloth (properly called "breechclout"), made with two yards of material between his legs and pulled up over a belt. It hung almost to the ground in the front and rear. The womens' garments included buckskin skirts, which were often two skins hung over a belt, in front and behind. A fringe was usually cut into the edges. The other basic item of clothing for both men and women was the moccasin. This was like a boot, turned over just below the knees. The folded over portion could be drawn up to protect the thighs. The soles of the moccasin were made of rawhide, the hairy side out, with a toe turned up about two inches in front to form a tab of various shapes. The print of the moccasin and its toe were unique to each of the various bands of Western Apache and Indian scouts could identify them on the trail.

The men in a family had three major occupations: hunting, raiding, and warfare. These activities gave meaning to the male Apache's life and provided necessary sustenance for the family. The men gathered about campfires, squatted under the trees or entered their sweat lodges to make plans for their hunts or raids. There were rituals to perform, dances to conduct and songs to sing. These were forms of prayer, designed to garner the power needed for the adventure. What booty they brought home from these events was turned over to the women of the camp to prepare, to process, to own and distribute, while the men rested and then prepared for their next manly activity.

Protecting the chastity and purity of women in the band was among the most serious of concerns for the men. The rape or seduction of one of the girls or women was ruthlessly avenged. Similarly, it was the fear of revenge that kept an Apache man from violating any woman not his own. This reciprocal vengeance and fear of vengeance established a high standard of sexual purity among the Apaches. However, widows were permitted more freedom and often would reward with sexual favors returning warriors who were single.

Marriage came early for the Apache girl and later for the male, who had to first prove his worthiness in raiding and hunting as a sign of his ability to support the extended family. She was ready for marriage after she began her menses and the time was marked by an elaborate puberty ceremony called "The Sunrise Dance." It is so named because it begins before sunrise. Though the girl must agree to perform her part, it is the family who decides the exact time for it to take place. They will need the help of their kinsmen for it is an elaborate and expensive celebration.

The relationships of boys and girls among the Apache were supervised closely. Even brothers and sisters were not left alone in camp, nor were courting couples allowed to be alone together. Courtship was conducted in public at the dances and food gathering parties, or working together in the fields. The partners chose each other, though sometimes the parents arranged the marriage. In that case, the boy's family carried his proposal to the girl's family in the form of gifts. The girl's family would gather and discuss it and divide the gifts among themselves if the proposal was accepted. If the proposal was rejected the gifts were returned. When a proposal was accepted the girl was sent to the boy's family camp, probably accompanied by a female relative. She slept with the boy's mother and sisters for several nights and on about the fourth day she could show her continued acceptance of the marriage by preparing breakfast for her intended groom. She then returned to her parents' camp where she and her mother built a *gowa* for them to live in. The boy then moved to her camp and the couple began living together. This act of living together was the extent of the marriage ceremony itself. Sometimes the *gowa* had been built before she went to the boy's camp and after her visit to his camp he simply returned with her to her camp to begin their new life together.

If the family did not arrange the marriage, the boy made the initial advance or the girl could choose her own husband. Selecting him frequently as a partner for the public dance became a sign to the community of their intentions and a way for the couple to communicate their intention to each other. When the boy made his bid for her, he took what he deemed the proper offering of gifts to her mother's *gowa* and left them there. A preferred gift was one or more horses, but the Tontos had few horses so it would more likely be buckskins, weapons, or spoils of the hunt. After four days if the gifts were still there or the horses unattended, the marriage would not proceed. If the gifts were accepted, or the horses cared for, the marriage was completed.

In Elliott Arnold's book *Blood Brother*, he describes a beautiful Apache wedding ceremony, which he had made up because, he said, "the truth was so boring." After all, it was a fictional book and he claimed the right to follow his imagination. The ceremony he created was so beautiful and touching that Apache couples often came to the Arizona Historical Society in Tucson for a copy, thinking it was genuine. In fact, there was no ritual for marriage other than the customs faithfully followed.

Chapter Twelve

TRAPPERS THREATEN APACHELAND

By the first half of the white man's 19th century, trail blazers were working around the fringe of Tonto lands. Explorers Garces, Beale, and Kearny traveled from east to west across the flat mesas in the north, utilizing the springs around today's Flagstaff, Arizona. To the south the Gila Trail passed through Tucson, blazed by the Mormon Battalion and the Butterfield Overland Stage. Both of these trails avoided the rugged mountains and foothills, canyons and forests, rims and valleys of central Arizona, and this allowed the Tonto Apaches to develop their lifestyle without reference to white men. Secluded as they were, Tonto Apaches could not know that the changing fashions of western civilization were about to affect them.

The rage among European and American men was to wear top hats, manufactured from beaver pelts that were felted. "Felting" is a process in which the fibers of the material are matted by pressure and rolling. The price of beaver pelts could go as high as $6 a pound in St. Louis and an average pelt weighed a pound and a half. That meant good money for those who dared to penetrate the wilds of America's western mountains and rivers. The French, English and Scottish trappers had already taken most of the available beaver in Canada and the northern Rocky Mountains. Furthermore, the monopolistic trading companies controlled their fur trappers, employing them with an annual salary. Men who called themselves free trappers were not content with such limits and looked to the untapped sources of beaver in the Southwest.

Around 1824 this new breed of men began to appear on the fringes of Tonto lands. Their skins were white but their language was incomprehensible to the Apaches because it was not Spanish. To add to the confusion, they dressed in the skins of animals, like Indians, wore moccasins, and preferred the company of natives to their own kind. They even took Indian wives, raised families and established kinship with various bands. These mountain men moved in stealth, like the Indians, and were so fierce it seemed wise for Apaches to befriend them, if only to find out what they were up to. These white men apparently hated the Mexicans as much as Apaches did and hope glimmered that they would become allies against a common enemy. In addition, the trappers were just passing through, utilizing the land as they went. They did not seem to have designs on the land itself.

The party of James Ohio Pattie followed the Gila River in 1826 from its headwaters to the Colorado River. During two such trips while skirting Apache territory they were harassed by Apaches and Pattie was almost killed in one skirmish by two arrow wounds. A few years later young Kit was in a party of trappers that followed the Verde River all the way north to the Mogollon Rim. On the way they engaged in a skirmish with Apaches in which twenty Indians were killed and many more wounded. Carson reported that they camped for three days "in the meadows and pine and aspen groves of the Black Forest where the Verde reaches up to drain the southern rim of the Mogollon Mesa." (Quoted in *Dear Old Kit: The Historical Christopher Carson*, edited by Harry L. Carter, University of Oklahoma Press, 1968) Carson's party had come very close to the Tonto stronghold. In dictating his life story, Carson said at this point, "We were nightly harassed by the Indians. They would frequently of nights crawl into our camp, steal a trap or so, kill a mule or horse and endeavor to do what damage they could." (*Kit Carson's Own Story of His Life*, Carson Memorial Foundation, Taos, New Mexico 1955 reprint, page 12). From there Carson and others of the party went on to California.

A little later the Mexican government in the state of Chihuahua offered a bounty for Apache scalps and a number of the trappers joined the hunt. A terrorist-type war developed around the fringes of the Tonto territory. While the Tontos kept as aloof as possible, it was a warning that even though their land was on the fringes of the white incursion they would soon have to fight. Some of the pressure was relieved when the dwindling finances of the Mexican Government caused the bounty to be withdrawn. Furthermore, the demand for beaver pelts slackened when Chinese and Japanese ports were opened to clipper ships in the 1840s and silk was being brought back to America. It soon replaced felted beaver as the top hat of choice.

In spite of explorations by the mountain men, the territory between the Rio Grande River and the Pacific Ocean was a mystery to Americans through most of the 1840s. That was about to change when, in May of 1846, the United States declared war on Mexico and a strong military force commanded by General Stephen Watts Kearny was marching west to capture California. His troops were aiming right for the central mountains of Arizona.

Chapter Thirteen

THE NOOSE TIGHTENS

By August of 1846 Kearny and his army had conquered Santa Fe, New Mexico and marched westward. On October 6th Kit Carson arrived at Kearny's camp, 150 miles from Santa Fe, with the news that California had fallen to the Americans without a fight. Carson was attached to an exploratory party headed by John C. Fremont. The other news he brought was not as encouraging. The most direct route for the Army of the West was through steep mountains with deadly drop-offs along narrow trails. It was impassible for wagons. The trail lacked the forage, water and game necessary to sustain Kearny's large force. However, a small party might cross and so Kearny sent most of his troops back to Santa Fe. Reducing his army to 110 men and retaining Kit Carson as guide, he determined to make a scientific study of the Gila River route. They proceeded to provide the first map and trail description leading directly toward Tonto Apache territory.

Kearny's troops marched into the Gila River valley, past Mount Graham, a holy mountain to all Apaches, and then into what twenty-four years later would be the location of Fort Apache and the San Carlos Indian Reservation. This was Western Apache country and a jumping-off place to the Tonto Apache homeland. Sometime between Oct. 26 and Nov. 7, the Kearny party encountered and dealt with a band of Indians who could have been Tonto, Cibecue, Pinal, or White Mountain Apaches. Probably eager to have the detachment continue on their way and desiring some of the trade items offered, the Indians supplied the mules needed sorely by Kearny. These Apaches were "decked-out in garb plundered from Mexicans." One of the Apache women who came in to trade "had on a gauze-like dress, trimmed with the richest and most costly Brussels lace, pillaged no doubt from some fandango-going belle of Sonora." (Reported by cartographer W. H. Emory (*Notes of a Military Reconnaissance: A Survey of Arizona Gila River, 1846*, Bob Cunningham, The Westerners "Smoke Signal" Tucson, Fall 1996). They also met a 12 year old Mexican boy who had been raised a slave by the Apaches, probably from babyhood, and who did not want to leave his Apache family. The Indians were mounted on stolen horses and these along with the mules bore witness to intensive raids on Mexicans by the Western Apaches.

Kearny proceeded down the Gila and observed the trail was well beaten and showed fresh signs of rustled cattle. The area where the San Pedro River enters the Gila was obviously a major raiding trail used by Western Apaches between Mexico and their strongholds. Further along the Army of the West was among the friendly Maricopa and Pima Indians and on to celebrations in California. White men had once again skirted the heartland of the Tontos.

In 1848, the war between the United States and Mexico ended with the treaty of Guadalupe Hidalgo, creating a new border between the two nations. That border was the Gila River from its headwaters in the mountains to the river's mouth near Yuma. Mexican and American authorities might have understood this imaginary borderline, but for the Apaches such an unseen border cutting through the heart of their traditional territory hardly made any sense. To complicate matters, the provisions of the treaty required the United States Army to prevent Apaches from raiding south of the Gila into Mexico. To make sure this provision was observed the United States was required to pay Mexican citizens for losses from raiders who invaded Mexico from the north. The United States attempted to negotiate treaties with Apache groups who lived along the border, but to no avail. Raids continued, especially near Tucson and Tubac, which were still below that international border.

During the next few years there was much activity along the east-west trails. Americans began a steady trek to California because of the gold rush. The United States Boundary Commission was surveying the new border with Mexico and over two-thirds of the U.S. Army was assigned to patrol that new border. Yet Indian raids increased, including those by Tonto Apaches. The road to California was littered with burned out wagons, the bones of slaughtered livestock, and the wayside graves of pioneers.

For Tonto Apaches, the growing traffic seemed like a noose around their necks, closing in on the fringes of their lands. Tonto raids now were far ranging, showing their desperation over incursions of the white men. In 1853 the Gadsden Purchase from Mexico was negotiated by the U. S. government and ratified in 1854, extending the southern border of the United States well below the Gila River. Such international politics were of little concern to the Tontos. All they knew was that the white men were tightening their grip on the areas they liked to raid in the south.

Chapter Fourteen

PRELUDE TO APACHE WARS

In the autumn of 1857, the United States began in earnest to develop a good road across northern Arizona. Edward Fitzgerald Beale surveyed and then built the pioneering wagon road from Fort Defiance, west of Albuquerque, to the Colorado River. As early as the summer of 1858 immigrants began using Beale's Wagon Road and, while they encountered many hardships, there are no records of Apache attacks along this route during those years. Tonto excursions into the white man's territory were concentrated in the south during the 1850s. It was there the action intensified, especially after the Butterfield Overland Stage line began regular runs across Arizona in 1858. This road not only crossed through the heartland of the Chiricahua Apaches, but cut the major raiding trails used by all the bands of Apaches in New Mexico and Arizona. Mining between the Gila River and the Mexican border was booming, bringing investors and laborers. To protect the settlers, military posts were increased, and in 1861 a skirmish at Apache Pass in the Chiricahua Mountains brought Cochise, his warriors, and his clans into a full scale war with the Americans. That same year America's Civil War broke out.

By 1862 the Tontos became aware that strange things were happening among their white adversaries. Word from their relatives in New Mexico and southern

Arizona told of American armies fighting among themselves. The Tontos could not understand this War Between the States, but it became evident that United States troops were being reduced and leaving their frontier posts. The Apaches concluded that their intensified raids during the 1850s had won them a victory and the white men were beginning to withdraw. The Indians took heart and became more ferocious than ever.

While America's Civil War raged, other events were taking shape that would directly affect the Tonto Apaches. In 1862 a well-seasoned gold hunter appeared along the Gila River headwaters. His name was Joseph Reddeford Walker. He was over 6 feet tall and strong, 200 pounds of bone and sinew to help him break trail along the rivers of the southwest. A beaver trapper from his early twenties, Walker was now 63. He had ranged the western mountains with his friend Kit Carson since 1820. The two of them were guides on the famous Fremont Expedition and Walker had honed his gifts of good judgment, strong will, nimble footing and physical strength. He would need them all as he became the first man to attempt the exploitation of Tonto Apache lands.

Joe Walker led a group of gold seekers from California into New Mexico and from Santa Fe they headed back west to explore the headwaters of the Gila River. By the fall of 1862 the Walker party was camped at the mine settlement of Pinos Altos, seven miles north of Silver City, New Mexico. The way west seemed blocked. Not only were bands of Apaches in control of the region, but the mountains were ominous and uninviting. Endless spines and crests with intermediate canyons rumpled and angled across their view in an endless maze, affording no passage. The terrain was too rocky and steep for man or beast to break through, especially while being harassed by Indians. They were well aware of Apache atrocities, for at one turn in the road they encountered three white men, dead, hanging by their ankles from a tree limb. Under their heads a fire smoldered which had literally cooked their brains. The gold seekers discovered Apaches had horses from the Spanish Entrada and guns from the more recent trappers. Even more significant, Apaches had a warfare tactic that consisted of stalking, harassing and luring the enemy into ambuscades. It was "like fighting ghosts," said Daniel Conner, a member of the party.

In January 1863, Walker had a plan. If he could capture an Apache chief, he might use him for safe passage while the party hacked their way westward into the mountains. Just such a person lived in the region of Pinos Altos, the infamous chief of the Warm Spring Mimbreno Apaches, Mangas Coloradas. Walker had the mistaken idea that there was a federation among all Apache tribes and this war chief was its headman. He concluded Mangas Coloradas would be a worthy hostage even among the Western Apaches.

Just then a contingent of California Volunteers, First Cavalry, arrived and camped with the Walker party. Some of their troops joined the civilians on the foray to capture the chief. They went to his stronghold, set out a white flag of truce and encouraged him to come to them under the ruse of making a treaty. When he appeared, the soldiers' guns were enough to persuade the chief to become their prisoner.

Back at Walker's camp, Mangas Coloradas was tethered and during the night army guards tortured him and goaded him into trying to escape. When he tried to run they shot him dead. Much to Walker's dismay the chief's head was scalped after the killing and his body dumped into a gully where it was buried the next day. A few days later, the body was exhumed, the head severed and boiled so the skull could be sent back East. Word of the atrocity traveled like the wind by runners and smoke signals, until far to the west even the Tonto Apaches had heard of it.

Chapter Fifteen

ARIZONA BECOMES A TERRITORY

After the death of Mangas Coloradas at the hands of soldiers and the Walker party, all possibility of entering Arizona's central mountains from the east was out of the question. The only route open to the gold seekers was to proceed south where they could join the Butterfield Trail. During their trek on February 24, 1863, President Abraham Lincoln signed an act separating Arizona Territory from New Mexico. This was done to keep the population of southern Arizona in the Union. However, the sights of the Walker party were not on the politics of that action but on the mountains in the north where they might find gold. They passed through Tucson in April and soon reached the Gila River that ran past the Pima and Maricopa Indian villages. These traditionally friendly people provided encouragement and native guides.

While there, a Pima war party returned from a raid on the Tontos. The Pima and Maricopa tribes were traditional enemies of the Tonto and Yavapai bands. The war party boasted a booty of deer hides and human scalps and while the warriors bragged how they had scalped the Apaches, the white men inquired as to how many scalps the Pimas had lost. The answer was, "Not one." The Apaches, they claimed, were "not brave enough" to take scalps. What the men of the Walker party did not know was that Apaches had strong beliefs that the ghost of the deceased remained with the scalp. Furthermore, they believed that when a person dies that soul takes the form the body had in death into the afterlife. Mutilation of an enemy's dead body was a means for Apaches to curse that person, but scalping was not a traditional act.

The Walker party continued to move west until they found a passageway north at the great bend in the Gila River. There a tributary entered that would lead them to mountains they could make out in the distance, a likely source of minerals. At first the river bed was dry, though later they heard the Indians call it *Haviamp*, meaning a place of big rocks and water. Europeans would mold that sound into Hassayampa. They enlisted the help of a Mojave chief named Irataba to guide them and none too soon for they encountered a band of Yavapai Indians who signaled for a meeting. The Indians had suddenly appeared "within ten paces," their bodies painted and their looks ferocious. Members of the Walker party were startled for they had not even realized they were being watched. Daniel Conner, one of the prospectors who kept and published a diary of their adventures, wrote, "These naked, barbarous wretches sneak out of their holes as insidiously as so many rats, and are not entitled to a consideration more dignified than that which is accorded to the rats and mice about the city livery stable." (*Joseph Reddeford Walker and the Arizona Adventure*, University of Oklahoma Press, 1956, page 88) Such attitudes set the tone for most white settlers and revealed a huge void in their understanding of the native culture.

The Yavapai would not give Irataba an assurance of safe passage and made threats regarding any further advance of the white men into their lands. The guide tried to talk Walker into turning back. When they insisted on proceeding, Irataba and his Mojaves left in the night. With great caution the party continued up the Hassayampa and established a camp about five miles from what would later become Prescott, Arizona. They proclaimed the area a mining district and made a compact as to how each member of the party would be assigned mining claims.

In May 1863 they returned to the Pima villages for supplies. While on the way the Walker party joined a group of prospectors from California, led by Abraham Peeples and guided by the well known mountain man Pauline Weaver. At this time they also included a Gila River rancher named King S. Woolsey. He had recently settled the Agua Caliente ranch and was known for his bravery in fighting off Indian raiders. Woolsey became one of the first to make a gold claim in the Walker district and the word went out causing Arizona's gold rush. The Walker and Peeples parties shared the mining districts around Prescott and become the first whites to penetrate the Yavapai and Apache territory of central Arizona.

Miners now came from far and wide and began establishing substantial camps, building log houses and laying in food from hunting expeditions while at the same time prospecting for new claims. A friendly band of Indians began visiting the camps, especially at meal times. There were frequent attempts by different groups of

Indians to approach the white men in camp, usually wanting to trade mescal for a mule or some other exchange. There were also encounters by the whites with lone Indians while out hunting, which sometimes resulted in trade but usually meant careful avoidance. The open war between the two groups had not yet been declared and the white men were wise enough not to assert their belief that "the only good Indian is a dead Indian."

Chapter Sixteen

THE CLASH OF CULTURES

When the newly appointed officials for the Territory of Arizona left New York on August 27, 1863 they were unsure of where they would go to establish the seat of territorial government. The logical choice would be Tucson, the more populous center of political influence. However, when they reached Santa Fe they read a newspaper account reporting rich gold strikes in the Weaver and Walker mining districts. They decided instead to establish the seat of government at a new fort being built near the growing mining camps. It was reasonable to locate in the center of the new territory.

Meanwhile, the miners around the Hassayampa River were prospecting in all directions. Included in their diaries was the first recorded entry of white men into the Verde River Valley, a border land between the Yavapai and Apache territories. These prospectors encountered a large number of Indian villages and were able to bluff their way through by shooting guns in the air and racing their mules through the center of the camps. One band withstood them and refused to run. The exchange of gunfire left all of the mules wounded as well as several of the men. The Indians pursued them until the white eyes were out of the valley. Coming over the mountain and back into grassland, the settlers encountered yet one more

Yavapai rancheria. It proved to be friendly and they rested there before returning to their permanent camp.

Companies of the California Infantry and Cavalry had set up a military post in Chino Valley, some miles north of the mining camps. It was named Whipple Barracks to honor Maj. General Amiel W. Whipple who had surveyed the route across northern Arizona and who had since been killed in the Civil War at the battle of Chancellorsville. It was to this post that President Lincoln's appointee, Governor Goodwin and his party, proceeded. They arrived there January 22, 1864 with plans to formulate the territorial government. In May the temporary capital was moved to a permanent location on Granite Creek, closer to the mining camps. Citizens immediately met to establish a town which they named Prescott to honor an eastern historian well known for his books about the Aztecs. (It was erroneously believed the Aztecs had been first settlers in the region.) Fort Whipple was also moved close to the village.

The growing intrusion of white mining camps and ranches into Yavapai lands bordering on Tonto territories brought an immediate response from the Indians. Territorial Judge Joseph Pratt Allyn, writing just two weeks after arriving at Ft. Whipple, had not yet made a distinction between Yavapai and Tonto Apache. They were alike to him. He wrote for his publisher, *The Hartford Evening Press*, "The Indians immediately about here are Tontos, or fool Apaches, the meanest and dirtiest Indians I have seen yet. Soon after my arrival a hundred or more of them came in to hold a council… and I think I never saw a more miserable set of human beings. In addition to the Tontos, the surrounding country is swept by the war-like Apaches of the country east. Stock is not safe anywhere, either in the mines or on the ranches; it has to be watched carefully in the daytime, and corralled at night. These repeated depredations have so thoroughly aroused the animosity of the settlers that a war of extermination has in fact already begun. Indians are shot wherever seen..."

One of the notable leaders of the war against the Indians was rancher King S. Woolsey. Woolsey had established his Agua Fria Ranch on one of the headwaters of the Agua Fria River, near today's Dewey, Arizona. This made his location the eastern-most outpost of white settlement. The Tonto and Yavapai Indians were delighted with such ranches in one sense, for it meant they would not have to travel so far south to secure livestock. On the other hand, they began to realize the seriousness of this threat to their hunting and gathering grounds.

On January 4, 1864, Tonto or possibly Yavapai raiders stole 33 head of cattle from Woolsey's Agua Fria ranch. Several settlers at Prescott lost 28 mules and horses. Altogether the ranchers and miners claimed several hundreds of animals stolen, enough to spur significant action. The citizens prevailed upon Woolsey to lead an expedition and three days later a group of about 40 private citizens set out after the raiders. They went south and then east along the Salt River and at some point in the Superstition Mountains they were confronted by a war party of Tontos. The chiefs were lured in for a conference and at a signal from Woolsey the whites pulled their guns and each shot the Indian beside him. A running battle ensued, with over thirty Indians and one white man dead. This skirmish came to be called the Bloody Tanks Massacre. It was the beginning of a nearly twenty year war against the Tonto Apaches.

Chapter Seventeen

INTO TONTO TERRITORY

King Woolsey and his militia returned from their Bloody Basin massacre to find the territorial governor, John Goodwin, calling for an exploratory party to enter the Verde River Valley to determine a good location for a new army post. The governor wanted further to explore the possibilities of mining and agriculture in that valley. In a meeting at Joe Walker's camp store, February 2, 1864, the governor spoke to a gathering of citizens. Judge Allyn was in the governor's party and wrote his impressions.

"This country is so infested with Apaches that prospecting has been impossible. During the evening, persons were constantly coming in who wished to join the party, one and all believing and talking of nothing but killing Indians. It is difficult to convey... an adequate idea of the intensity of this feeling. A miner seems to regard an Indian as he would a rattlesnake...The governor, in a brief speech, took all by storm by advocating the extermination of the Indians..." (*The Arizona of Joseph Pratt Allyn*, John Nicholson ed., University of Arizona Press, Tucson, 1974, page 70, 76).

Woolsey's Agua Fria ranch became the rendezvous point for the expedition into the Verde Valley. As the large party assembled the hills echoed with reports from their long rifles as they target practiced. There were fifty soldiers and about fifteen civilians, including the aging mountain man Pauline Weaver, prospector Joseph Walker, King Woolsey, Judge Allyn, and the governor. After several days of preparations and packing a large mule train the expedition set off on Sunday, February 21, 1864. It was the first official military march against the Tonto and Yavapai tribes.

After several failed attempts to cross the mountains and find a passageway into the valley, they finally reached the Verde River four days later and enjoyed excellent fishing for their supper. Indians hooted at them during the night and lurked just outside their camps. One Indian brave they met tried to hold them off with his bow and arrow while his wife and baby attempted to escape. Gunfire killed the little family. Indians now appeared all around the whites who were shooting wildly in every direction. An arrow wounded one of the soldiers, 24 year old Private Joseph Fisher. He died before a detachment could carry him back to Fort Whipple. He was the first American soldier to die in this new war against the Tonto Apaches.

King Woolsey then led a scouting party north and east along the river. They detected signs of stolen livestock and knew they were in the area of the raiders. Woolsey's party continued north as far as Oak Creek and returned with reports of luxuriant grass and water. Late that day, two Mexican boys arrived breathlessly in camp from Woolsey's Agua Fria ranch to report that 60 Indians had raided the ranch in broad daylight. They had taken all of

Woolsey's livestock except the oxen that were plowing near the house. He could do little about it at that moment and the lure of this expedition kept him from immediately returning home. However, Woolsey resolved to organize another scout against the Tontos as soon as he returned and penetrate their lands to the east.

Before returning home the party explored ancient ruins in the Verde Valley, supposing them to be left by some great Aztec invasion that had once subjected the Apaches in that area. They bestowed on one of the ruins the name Montezuma's Castle. Exploring south along the river they noted the area around the mouth of Clear Creek would be an excellent location for an outpost and readily irrigated for farming. Going further to the south they found the East Fork of the Verde where traces of gold brought vows to return and prospect up that river.

While near the East Fork of the Verde the civilian party brazenly attacked a Tonto Apache camp but was driven off by the Indians. For the next seven days the soldiers and civilians struggled south along the Verde River leaving their worn out mules behind one by one. The Tonto bands, well alerted to this invasion, sent smoke signals to report the impending danger throughout Tonto territory.

At last, on March 11, the explorers emerged from the wilderness and into the desert on the lower Verde River. Judge Allyn parted company to visit the Pima villages and the governor with the rest of the party headed back to Ft. Whipple. Woolsey was eager to return home and begin organizing a second crusade into Tonto territory which he would lead.

This time General Carlton gave the all-civilian militia his blessing and a 30-day supply of rations from Ft. Whipple. Their departure was delayed while they waited for the supplies but on March 29th, at ten o'clock at night, the expedition left Woolsey's Agua Fria ranch. It would be the white man's first successful march all the way across the land claimed by the Tonto Apaches.

Chapter Eighteen

CROSSING TONTO LAND, Part A

Tonto Apaches had raided the ranches around Prescott and an expedition of civilians was organized to pursue the raiders in hopes of killing them and recapturing the cattle. They got started on the night of March 29, 1864, and trekked down the Agua Fria River. In several running gun battles with a cluster of Yavapai camps they killed over thirty Indians. The appointed secretary of the group, Henry Clifton, wrote, "After the fight was over we commenced hunting the brush to see how many we had bagged..." To these men the Indians were simply varmints to be killed at every opportunity. They believed they were justified when the Yavapai camps yielded the tails of horses and mules as well as hides that carried the brands of ranchers in the party.

We are indebted to at least two eyewitness accounts for the details of King Woolsey's expedition as it continued into the Rim Country during the spring of 1864. One account was given by Henry Clifton, whose notes were printed in the Prescott *Arizona Miner* on May 11th and 25th. The more detailed account comes from the diary of F. A. Cook, one of the participants. His original diary is in the Sharlot Hall Museum in Prescott, Arizona.

After their foray against the Yavapai camps, Woolsey's army rested and healed their bruised feet before moving on to the Verde Valley. Because this was their second venture into the Verde Valley they knew the best route to take. After crossing the Verde River they ascended Clear Creek Canyon a distance of six miles. The Mogollon Rim is such a maze of canyons it was impossible for the Tonto bands to always know their enemy's movements. Woolsey's party surprised one small Tonto family that was camped and roasting mescal (the hearts of the agave plant, a staple Apache food). The Apaches were able to escape into the forest but the running gun battle alerted the entire region. After that, the Tontos and Yavapai made sure the would-be soldiers did not catch a glimpse of them. In fact, the Indians were entertained from their secluded watch-posts by the sight of white men getting lost time after time in the chasms. The white men could not replenish their water without descending into the depths of Clear Creek Canyon and this hampered their progress.

Although the rancherias they came upon were deserted the militia destroyed the Apache's food stores. The Tontos would surround the white men's camp at night and shoot arrows at them as soon as the men rose in the morning. On April 8th one of the party, J. Donohugh, was struck by an arrow that passed between his jugular vein and windpipe, protruding out the other side. The physician accompanying the invaders, John T. Alsap, was able to extract the arrow so that Donohugh recovered.

As the Woolsey party advanced they gave names to landmarks as though these storied places had no history before this. The Apaches had very descriptive names for these same places, each carrying a rich tradition passed on from generation to generation. However, the names given by Woolsey are the ones that have come down to us. A favorite camp of both Yavapai and Tonto Apache had been along a creek whose springs put forth water at a consistent 72 degrees. The Woolsey party observed how that warm water leeched the limestone rock through which it flowed and left a crystallized coating on whatever it touched. Branches, leaves and stones acquired a fossil-like appearance and so Woolsey named it Fossil Creek.

The Woolsey party was very thorough in their exploration of the basins, mesas and canyons that spread across the foot of the Mogollon Rim. The Tontos must have felt secure, however, in their fortress-like territory and probably laughed among themselves at the cumbersome way these invaders conducted their scouting parties. The supply train of 60 mules was especially enticing to Indians who relished mule meat. The warriors followed the progress closely as the muleskinners tried without success to locate a potential wagon route eastward. On the night of June 6th the white militia camped on a flood plain beside the East Verde River. They were probably at the future location of the LF Ranch, an area later settled by the Chilson, Taylor, and Pyeatt families. The field contained stalks of Apache corn from the previous autumn. Signal fires burned brightly on the surrounding hills and the Apaches drew close enough to yell from the hilltops at the supply train. The Indians had sense enough to stay just out of gunshot. Their purpose was to worry the whites.

When the Woolsey party came to the mouth of Pine Creek they went over a low divide heading southeast and followed a stream Woolsey named Wild Rye because of the grasses that were growing. On June 7th they reached the junction of Rye Creek with a larger river which they named Tonto Creek. This was the territory of the powerful Tonto headman Del-che-ae (also Delshay). Already the Woolsey party had penetrated Tonto territory farther than white men had ever ventured before.

Chapter Nineteen

CROSSING TONTO LAND, Part B

As King Woolsey and his citizen army continued to invade Tonto Apache territory the Indians observed how these men would scramble up the hillsides with their picks and dip their pans into the streambeds. It was strange behavior not understood by the Tontos for whom this procession of white men was a terrible inconvenience, disrupting their lifestyle. They had to put aside hunting and gathering activities, to say nothing of social dances, in order to follow these bearded, heavily clothed people. They had to abandon their villages and camps and then after the whites moved on they returned to assess the damage. The invaders destroyed the food stores and crops at the Tonto camps.

After exploring the northern reaches of Tonto Creek Woolsey found the creek took an abrupt turn toward the southeast, flowing through a basin bordered by several mountain ranges. The mouth of Tonto Creek emptied into the Salt River and the conjoined rivers broke through the mountains, racing down canyons toward the desert valley. What Woolsey's crew called Cottonwood Camp was a paradise for Tonto Apaches. Here a Tonto band lived peacefully alongside a Pinal Apache band. Many old and new wickiups were about the area as were the ruins of ancient pueblo and mound dwellers. The

Apaches had made good use of the tools left behind by the earlier people.

Not far back up the Tonto Basin beaver dams formed a refreshing lake. Only the white man's superior firepower kept the Indians at bay while the intruders fished and swam, hunted and feasted. The Apache taboo on fish resulted in an abundance of very large fish in Tonto Creek and the Salt River. F. A. Cook wrote, "We made a willow drag and caught about 200 fish. The largest ones looked very much like cod but had no teeth and would weigh from 10 to 20 pounds. This kind of fishing was new to many of us, but was very fine sport for we had to go into the river and in some places it was up to our necks. But the weather was very hot and the waters warm."

It was June 17th when they broke camp and headed up the Salt River. The Woolsey army had now moved out of Tonto Apache territory and into that of the Pinal Apaches. The invaders followed the streams and stayed near the springs while the Apaches burned signal fires on the surrounding hills and yelled indistinguishable words from a distance. Several times Indian emissaries carrying white flags actually approached the white men's camp ostensibly to beg for food. It was a clever Apache custom to enter an enemy camp under a flag of truce to assess its strength before an attack. In this case the attack did not come, probably because the rag-tag army continued to pass through and their firepower was superior. They went as far as the newly established Fort Goodwin near the Gila River and entered White Mountain Apache territory. They prospected up the Black River, one of the headwaters of the Salt River. All during this time the various tribes of Western Apaches were attentive to Woolsey's militia. The awful tales of Spanish atrocities, scalps for pesos bartered by white trappers, and the tortured death of chief Mangas Coloradas by the army with the Walker party the year before were told around Apache campfires. The Apaches must have known this invasion boded evil for them.

It was nearing the end of July when the men, now more interested in gold than stolen cattle, turned homeward. While still in White Mountain Apache territory, the Indians drew first blood. One of the party, J. W. Beauchamp, went to the top of a mountain to survey the surrounding country. A band of Apaches waylaid him, shot, lanced, stripped and left him for dead. He lived for some 20 minutes after his cohorts reached him but died before they could return to camp. "We buried him at the foot of the mountain," wrote Woolsey in his report, "which we named Beauchamp Peak in memory of the unfortunate victim of Indian cruelty and cowardice."

By mid-August the party was back in Tonto territory and camped near the mouth of Tonto Creek. There one of the party, O. Allen, accidentally discharged his gun and killed a fellow camper, Gaston Moreal. Woolsey does not mention this in his report, probably embarrassed that two of his men were killed on the tour but his citizen army had no success in killing Tonto Indians in their own land. The party retraced their way up Tonto Creek and the Rye Creek drainage. Then once on the East Verde River they followed it to its mouth, through the rugged wilderness west of today's Payson. Throughout these days the Apaches shouted and rolled rocks down from the high cliffs. No one was hurt and shots from the white men's rifles usually scattered the warriors.

The Indians were so invisible the white men had no idea how many there were and Woolsey underestimated the tenaciousness of the Tonto Apaches. His report to the governor contained this evaluation, "We have followed the trail of the Apache to his home in the mountains and have learned where it is located. We have dispelled the idea of vast numbers that has ever been attached to that tribe. A few hundred poor, miserable wretches compose the formidable foe so much dreaded by many. They will be brought to terms speedily, or exterminated, I cannot doubt, when once the government shall know how small is the enemy by which so much annoyance has been caused."

To bring the central mountains of Arizona under white control would take the next twenty years.

Chapter Twenty

THE INFANTRY INVADES

The Woolsey party did not accomplish any of their immediate goals: to kill Indians, find gold or recover lost livestock. However, they did follow the Tonto Basin its entire length and explore as far east as the San Carlos and Black Rivers. They brought back to Prescott glowing reports of the Apache country. In his report to the governor Woolsey said, "The whole country through which we have passed is covered with excellent grass. Water is plentiful for all ordinary purposes. In many places beautiful little valleys invite the farmer and rancher to follow the occupation of their choice. We never found gold in any paying quantities and yet I cannot help thinking that there is in that part of the country great mineral wealth."

Settlers were itching to take possession after that. Sensing the threat, Tonto Apaches intensified their raids on ranches and wagon trains around the fringes of the central mountains. By 1865 the demands of the settlers for protection reached a fever pitch. Arizona was hard put for cash but the governor called for raising a volunteer army to protect the interests of the new territory. Such militias were to be mustered into the United States Army as infantry units. It is notable that the white men who cried the loudest for protection were loath to join the volunteers. Less than five full companies were raised and the great majority of those who enlisted were Mexicans as well as Pima and Maricopa Indians. They were the natural enemies of the Apaches and readily responded to a promise of regular pay, food and arms. As it would turn out, there was not enough food, arms or clothes to supply the volunteer infantry. Troops had to march with feet bound in rags or homemade buckskin moccasins. Hunting wild game was often their only sustenance. Yet, the companies made an indelible mark as they became the first military front to oppose the Tonto Apaches.

A plan for the defeat of the Tonto Apaches was put in place by the army. 7th Infantry and 1st Cavalry Volunteers from California were sent to establish a military post seven miles up the Verde River from its confluence with the Salt River. Their orders were to locate the post somewhere deep in Tonto territory, perhaps in the Tonto Basin or Sierra Ancha areas. However, their commander realized the mountains formed too great a barrier for the movement of a large force into the Tonto stronghold and so Ft. McDowell was established as "a temporary post" until it could be moved north. Two companies of Arizona Volunteers were assigned to join the troops at Camp McDowell. They were Company C with just under 100 Pima Indians and Company B with 94 Maricopa Indians. Among the Pima Company was their chief, Antonio Azul, who was made first sergeant.

It was September 15th when the Tontos received their first challenge from the newly established army post. Their lookouts failed to spot the white and Indian volunteers moving up Sycamore Creek and over the Mazatzal Mountains. White soldiers were not able to surprise the Tontos but now with Pima and Maricopa scouts the element of stealth was added to the maneuvers. The Indian scouts were issued red and blue shirts, blue pants, and red bandannas for their heads. In this way the soldiers could distinguish them from the Apaches. A rancheria about nine miles east of today's Payson (possibly at Little Green Valley or Diamond Point) experienced a surprise attack at dawn. The Tontos were quick to escape into the forest, though one was killed and several wounded. The troops looted and burned the village, returning to McDowell on September 19th. A few weeks later an Apache band was routed near the mouth of Tonto Creek and five were killed, eight captured. On October 15th three Tontos were killed but by November 24th when a six day expedition left McDowell, the Apaches were well warned by their lookouts. This time the army failed to locate them.

As the attacks from both sides escalated, Apache rancherias were destroyed, their men and youth killed, the women and children taken prisoner. The Arizona Volunteers usually sold these captive children to white and Mexican families for slave labor. The regular soldiers for their part were carrying trophies of their attacks back to camp, such as Apache scalps, ears and even genitals. The Tontos responded with their own forms of warfare. They made small and incredibly sharp arrowheads of obsidian, a black volcanic glass, or of chert. When such an arrow struck the bone, its brittle head would shatter or detach from the shaft and remain in the body when the arrow was pulled out. Sometimes the arrowhead was poisoned with deer liver left in the sun to putrefy, then injected with rattlesnake venom.

By this time another military post had been established to the west of the Tontos in the Verde Valley. The growing strength of the white armies now put such pressure on the Indians they began to join forces. The Yavapai bands along the Verde and Hassayampa Rivers abandoned their ground and moved east to ally with the Tonto Apache chiefs, one of the best known being the powerful Del-che-ae.

Chapter Twenty-One

A PINCERS ON THE TONTOS

While the Tontos were being attacked by troops from Fort McDowell on the south a new threat loomed from the west. A colony of white settlers had begun farming the bottomlands of Clear Creek in the Verde River Valley. Since this area was the informal borderland between the Tonto and Yavapai bands, the new white settlement was encroaching where both tribes claimed sovereignty. A second colony of farmers soon moved into the valley establishing farms a few miles north at the mouth of Beaver Creek. The Indians enjoyed both of these communities as a handy source of grain and livestock and the settlers pressed the government for protection. Their pleas were answered by a military presence at the end of August, 1865 when a detachment of New Mexico Volunteers from Ft. Whipple set up a camp near the Clear Creek settlement. As they were descending into the Verde Valley three hundred warriors armed with rifles, bows and arrows attacked them. Though none of the soldiers was killed, many of their supplies and records, as well as the surgeon's wagon, were burned, and their horses driven off. The tattered detachment of soldiers arrived at the Verde River settlements on foot, in spite of being a cavalry unit, and was of little help other than the threat to the Indians by their physical presence.

Ten days later the Tontos raided the cornfields, escaping up Beaver Creek and scattering on top of the Mogollon Rim. The soldiers, two civilian guides and six of the citizens pursued the raiders but after marching a grueling eleven miles into the mountains they gave up and returned home. The Indian raids on settlers' cornfields continued to increase as the crop ripened for harvest. Literally, scores of Indians would come down the canyons from the east and the fields became the site of numerous skirmishes, wounds and deaths on both sides.

In October, Company A of Arizona Volunteers from Prescott arrived to bolster the camp and lift the morale of both civilians and army. They brought with them a sweeping declaration of war from General Mason who had visited Ft. Whipple. "All Apache Indians in this Territory are hostile and all men large enough to bear arms who may be encountered will be slain wherever met, unless they give themselves up as prisoners. All rancherias, provisions and whatever of value belonging to the Indians that may be captured, will be destroyed, except such articles as may be of value to the United States, which will be turned in to the proper officers and duly accounted for."

Acting Governor Richard McCormick in his December 1865 message to the Second Territorial Legislature expressed the prevailing attitude of the whites. "For the relentless Apache by whose hands so many of our patient pioneers have fallen, whose hostile presence is... the chief obstacle to the growth and development of the Territory..., utter subjugation, even to extermination, is admitted as a necessity by all who are familiar with (the Apache's) history and habits... It is the primary and all important work to which our attention must be given."

More gentle voices, such as Army surgeon Elliott Coues, were drowned in the clamor for Apache genocide. Coues wrote from Fort Whipple, "We are fighting Apaches continually, killing a few only to stir up the rest to renewed atrocities... (If we would) treat the Indian as if he were a human being (it would) encourage him to return the favor."

In the month of December the post on the Verde River was named Camp Lincoln to honor the martyred President. Early that month a severe two-day snowstorm hit the Tonto Basin and its surrounding mountains. The Tontos were hard pressed to find food, especially since the continuing attacks from Camps Lincoln and McDowell were destroying their crops and caches of food. Scouts from McDowell observed Apaches scraping the snow in search of seeds. In spite of the severe weather an army scouting party crossed the Mazatzals and Tonto Creek and marched into the Sierra Ancha. The Tontos knew they were coming and abandoned their rancherias but their tracks in the snow encouraged the troops to continue the pursuit. However, the army horses were becoming lame and the soldiers' shoes and clothing wearing out. Most of the scouts and soldiers returned to the post empty handed. The harassing invasions continued and since their pursuers trapped the Tontos the Indians were unable to escape the cold by moving to lower ground, as was their custom in winter.

During one raid into what would later be called Greenback Valley, Lt. William Hancock found a $100 bill and a soldier's letter in one of the wickiups. A Tonto Apache had apparently stashed it after a raid on a mail courier. Before the detachment returned to Camp McDowell they attacked another rancheria killing one woman and taking seven prisoners. The commander proudly reported the entire foray had netted 18 Tontos dead and 15 prisoners.

Chapter Twenty-Two

THE BATTLE OF FIVE CAVES

After the snow melted, the army moved Camp Lincoln in the Verde Valley three miles north to the settlement at the mouth of Beaver Creek. This location was on higher ground and the army hoped both the upper and lower communities could have better protection from this point.

In January 1866, while Camp Lincoln was being relocated, the all-Mexican Company E of the Arizona Volunteers marched from Ft. Whipple to the Verde Valley. Wind and thunderstorms made their trip unusually long and the bedraggled company arrived on January 16th with "their feet tied up in rags...," reported the post surgeon Dr. Edward Palmer. " The condition of these men was wretched beyond description."

The Apaches, lurking in the nearby forest, gleefully noted the soldiers' poor condition. They had no pack animals so it seemed they could not pursue the Indian raiders. At Camp Lincoln there were no buildings to shelter the troops and they had to live in handmade dugouts or caves on the edge of the mesa where a steep bluff descended to the creek below. However, the Mexican soldiers were eager to pursue their old enemy and to collect the $100 bonus each of them was promised at the end of their one year of service.

The company of California Infantry, which had been stationed at Camp Lincoln, left on January 31st. Captain Hiram S. Washburn of the Arizona Volunteers took command of the post at that time.

The Verde River is fed by several major streams flowing west from the Mogollon Rim. These are Oak Creek, Beaver Creek, Clear Creek, the East Fork of the Verde, and Fossil Creek. Each of these streams creates a canyon leading into the rugged mountains and when the soldiers pursued the Tontos up these canyons they found themselves confronted by a labyrinth of trails in an endless forest. The Indians moved more rapidly than the soldiers did and could spread out in their well-known territory. The soldiers packed their rations and blankets on their backs and these burdens, together with the fact that they had no shoes and wore homemade moccasins, made travel difficult. During their first scout against the Tontos on January 26th the soldiers discovered their moccasins lasted only four days on the trail. The Indians were well warned and watched from their secluded posts as Company E returned to Camp Lincoln empty handed.

In the middle of February the Tontos suffered the largest massacre of their people to that date at the hands of the Volunteers from Camp Lincoln. A band, or extended family, was living in a series of five caves clustered on the side of a deep canyon near the headwaters of Beaver Creek. On present day maps this was probably near Apache Maid in the Coconino Forest. The stealthy Volunteers, in their quiet moccasins, surprised the Tontos at dawn on February 15, firing into the caves from different directions so that the shots would ricochet off ceilings and walls. The air was filled with bullets and arrows, the shouts of soldiers and the screams of wounded Apaches.

The leader of the Volunteers, Lt. Manuel Gallegos, called in Spanish for the Tontos to surrender. They yelled back that they would rather die first, which all but a few did in the battle that followed. After three hours, thirty Apaches lay dead, twelve were taken prisoner, and two were seen to escape. Six of the troopers were wounded, though none was killed.

Dr. Edward Palmer said, "The caves presented a horrible sight, as dead of all ages and sexes, with household goods and provisions, lay mixed with the dirt from the caves brought down by firing of the guns while the blood of the dead freely mixed with all."

The soldiers were apparently not as overwhelmed as Dr. Palmer by the sight and plundered the goods and buckskins that were in the caves. The twelve Tonto prisoners included two adult women and ten children. One of the children died from a wound soon after reaching Camp Lincoln. The laundresses and mistresses in the camp baptized the dead child along with the other captured children according to their Catholic faith. Then they held a funeral service in a secret place and buried the child. The burial was in secret because the soldiers and women learned Dr. Palmer wanted the child's body for "a specimen," and would send the bones back to the Smithsonian Institution.

The other children were sold into slavery and the Battle of the Five Caves was heralded among the Americans as a great victory in Arizona's Indian War. Lt. Gallegos and his company gained praise in the newspapers as having "in one scout, while his men were without shoes, and living on half rations, killed more Indians in three hours than all the other (soldiers) in the Territory killed in the past year." The governor and Third Territorial Legislature also joined in the plaudits.

After that, the Tontos increased their attacks in the Verde Valley. When one of the soldiers went fishing, hoping to supplement their meatless diet, he was murdered by three Apache warriors and stripped of his clothing and ammunition.

Chapter Twenty-Three

THE NATURAL BRIDGE DISCOVERED

Throughout 1866 the Tonto Apache War escalated as troops from Camp Lincoln and Fort McDowell increased their forays into the Mogollon Rim country, its foothills and the Tonto Basin. Villages were burned, newspaper reports victoriously announced twenty Indians killed here, ten there, a dozen another time, then again twenty-five. It was clear to the Tontos that their small family bands had become like wild game to the invaders. Fortunately, their life style of mobility made it easy for them to elude the soldiers, but they retaliated by ambushing soldiers as they traveled and attacking army supply trains in the south.

In the spring the Volunteer army from Camp Lincoln made another foray into the Tonto territory all the way from the Tonto Basin to the Little Colorado River. No sooner did the company return than they were sent eastward again. After crossing the Black Mesa (Mogollon Rim) along now familiar canyon trails, they descended following Pine Creek. The explorers sighted numerous smoke signals as Apaches warned one another of the approaching troops and eventually they came to what today is the Tonto Natural Bridge State Park. From the high, overlooking hills they saw there a rancheria with Indians moving about. This is the first recorded discovery by Americans of the Natural Bridge.

Gallegos sent one party around behind the Tonto camp and waited with the remainder of his troops to cut off their retreat. The scouting party encountered an Indian and shot him. That alerted the others who fled as the troops then advanced to scorch the abandoned rancheria. Gallegos reported, "I sent four soldiers with the two who had shot the aforesaid Indian, and they had to give him three more shots before killing him entirely, for he was fortified among some rocks and defended himself to the last." They did capture one old man who was hiding among the rocks. He informed them there had been five men, one woman, and a child in this band and that they had only been at this place two days, fleeing from another force along the (East Verde) River. It was probably a detachment from Fort McDowell. The company took their prisoner, retraced their march and arrived back at Camp Lincoln in the afternoon of July 20th.

The old Tonto Apache confessed that his people were completely demoralized by the constant pursuit and no longer knew where to flee for safety. The pitiful old fellow became the butt of jokes by the troops in camp and Dr. Palmer recounts his fate. "For a long time a paymaster had been expected at Camp Lincoln, so as the scout returned they palmed off the prisoner as the paymaster that had been looked for, for so long a time. These troops had not been paid since they entered the army. Many had come to the conclusion they would get nothing for their service... As no paymaster came through, in spite of plenty of promises, the soldiers concluded that this poor dried up old Indian, without a tooth and almost naked, was as good a paymaster as they would see. By that name he was called as long as he was in Camp. He was allowed his freedom about Camp by day, as he was quite lame, but at night he had to sleep in the guard house.

"One morning he was missing. Search was made. He was said to be found in a ravine. As he was nearly blind, as well as lame, he missed the footpath and as he reached the (ravine) fell in and so injured himself that he must soon die. They having no means to remove him to Camp... the discharge from a rifle was thought to be the best and most charitable way of ending his extreme sufferings..."

Palmer's interpretation is difficult to believe, especially when Captain Washburn's account says the prisoner tried to escape, was pursued, then leaped down a steep bluff and was killed. One has to ask, if it had been a white man or a soldier lying in that ravine whether he would have been shot as "the most charitable way of ending his extreme sufferings."

The Tontos took advantage of the monsoon that drenched the American troops nearly every day that July. Many of them, including Lt. Gallegos, were too sick to effectively pursue raids and the Indians intensified their stealing of grain from the Clear Creek settlement. By early August the Volunteers at both Camp Lincoln and Fort McDowell were being mustered out of the service, as their terms were expiring, and no level of government had funded an extension. The Tontos began to sense victory, as reflected in this letter by Capt. Washburn to Col. W. H. Garvin, Sept. 12, 1866. "The Indians are now harvesting the corn at this settlement at the rate of about 30 or 40 bushels nightly. There is but one soldier left who is able to shoulder a musket, and he has charge of the commissary stores at this Camp, what there are; no meat left. When the bearer of this leaves, there will be two citizens left who call themselves well. I am hourly expecting an attempt to take the stock. I have to do guard duty day and night. If assistance does not come very soon, I shall have to abandon what government property I am trying to protect, and shall seek security for myself and animals."

Chapter Twenty-Four

TALK OF PEACE

The summer of 1866 found the soldiers at Ft. McDowell plagued by bronchitis, dysentery and scurvy, resulting in several deaths. Blame was put on the lack of fruits and vegetables so an effort was made to develop a farm near the post. The "bronchitis" was actually valley fever. To add to the problems, the Arizona Volunteer units of Pimas and Maricopas were becoming restless as their enlistment was running out and they had not received their promised pay. Tonto Yavapai bands sensed the onset of weakness at the garrison and sent a messenger saying they wished to make peace.

The post commander accepted their invitation and met with a large group of Tontos ten miles east of the post. The Indians responded to his good will by accompanying the soldiers back to McDowell where two days of negotiations took place. The commander invited the Tonto leaders to bring their people in and settle near the post and they would be furnished rations. In response, about four hundred and fifty warriors with forty women and children came to set up camp. They reported that about two thousand other Tontos wanted to come in also. Because their food stores had been so decimated by the soldiers they were hungry and sick.

However, during the next few days rumors spread among the Tontos that what the army really wanted was to observe and control them. On the night of August 18th the entire company of Indians vanished. The commander knew the army had to establish outposts deeper into Tonto territory and after waiting almost a week he sent an infantry detachment to forge a route over the Mazatzal Mountains. Heading to the Tonto Basin, they followed Sycamore Creek to Sunflower Valley, then proceeded northeast around Mt. Ord along an old Indian trail to Tonto Creek. Crossing the creek they climbed into the Sierra Ancha (Spanish for "wide mountain") where they burned deserted Tonto rancherias and gathered up usable food and hides. Since their shoes were worn out they returned to the post.

After the Tonto bands stayed at Ft. McDowell the post surgeon, Dr. Smart reported a vivid description of the Tonto people. "Their average height is about five feet four or five inches. They are slimly built and possess but little muscular development, yet they are very agile, climbing the mountains with great rapidity, and running on more level ground for many miles without any semblance of fatigue. The skin is of a light brownish-red color... They have generally the traits well marked of the American Indian; some, however, have a full round face and Chinese cast of countenance. The head is covered with a mass of rusty black hair, cut off in front on a level with the eyebrows, and permitted to grow a little longer behind, but never reaching the shoulders; occasionally the hair is worn quite short, round head cut. The beard, when any does grow, is dragged out hair by hair, by means of an elongated piece of tin, formed into a forceps by being bent lengthwise of itself, and which is usually carried suspended from the neck by a thong of buckskin...

"With one exception they were not painted. The paint in the exceptional case was of a grayish white color, and laid on in lines, narrow, closely set, and wavy, transverse and parallel, covering the face, chest and back. Their dress consists of the breechcloth and a pair of buckskin moccasins. The latter have a stout hard sole, which curves upwards a little in front of the toes; poorer specimens only cover the ankles, but others are so long that when drawn up they encase the thighs. This, with a leather bracelet on one wrist and a bow and quiver of arrows, forms the general outfit. But others are more completely equipped, wearing a buckskin thrown over one shoulder and fastened in the opposite armpit, and perhaps possessing a waist-belt of leather and an old sheath-knife, the product of probably some Sonora enterprise..."

"None wore any covering for the head with the exception of the chief whose crown consisted of a closely fitting skull-cap of skin, unadorned behind, but covered in front with feathers and many spangles of brass and tin. He also possessed a doublet of prepared buckskin, brownish red in color, with some blue linen markings on it... In disposition, they seem to be light-hearted, but subject to sudden fits of suspicion and timidity, which is perhaps sufficiently accounted for by the active campaign of late kept up against them..."

Throughout the fall of 1866 the soldiers from McDowell carried an intense campaign into the Sierra Ancha. Many natives were killed, taken prisoner, and their villages destroyed. The Tonto bands were shocked to realize that even their most secluded camps were vulnerable to white attack. The Military Department of the Pacific sent orders that an army post should be established in the center of the Tonto stronghold. However the mountains were so rugged the soldiers often found themselves ambushed while Apache signal fires burned from every surrounding hill. It was determined impossible to build a wagon road into the Sierra Ancha and any outpost should be built west of those mountains.

Meanwhile the raids on Indian camps were celebrated in the territorial newspapers and Major General Henry Halleck, commander of the Division of the Pacific, expressed confidence that a forced peace was possible by "a hunt of extermination."

Chapter Twenty-Five

CHIEF DELSHAY APPEARS

In October, 1866 a dramatic event occurred at Ft. McDowell. The most formidable of the Tonto Apache chiefs presented himself. His name was Del-che-ae, and accompanying him was his band of one hundred warriors, forty women and sixty children. The women and children were a sign he wanted peace. He also brought several headmen and their bands. His name was similar to the name by which the Tontos called themselves, De-he'ch-ahe. Del-che-ae, which translates Red Ant, was a young chief of considerable influence among the Tonto and Yavapai bands. His name is spelled many ways, but when Americans referred to him, they simply spelled it *Delshay*.

The long winter stretched ahead and many of the food stores of his people had been destroyed. The young chief knew he must seek help. Delshay emerged very suddenly to the white-eyes, like a thundercloud that erupts with a change in the wind. He would be the one who did not yield, though what we know of him must come from the record of his white enemies since his own people did not write. They told stories and Delshay lived in those stories told around campfires until campfires gave way to gas stoves and the stories were heard no more. The elders took most of their history to the grave. Today their children's children are seldom taught to speak the language but these latter day Tontos would be proud of Del-che-ae, The Red Ant.

Perhaps he was named for a hill of red ants at the place he was born. Perhaps it was the stinging bite of his fighting spirit that gave him the name. Perhaps the name pointed to his special power to lead and to work hard, a power he gained when he passed from childhood to manhood. Whatever the reason, his name enabled the Tonto Apaches to hold their head high during the decade of the 1860s. Delshay became the cause of chilling fear among the white soldiers. He was born in the Mazatzal Mountains around 1835 to 1840 but his stronghold was in the Sierra Ancha. After a mortal encounter with a white man, he took a pearl shirt-stud from the victim and wore it in his left ear. This made him very distinguishable to the U.S. military.

When he appeared at Fort McDowell asking to discuss an alliance he showed that he had little understanding of America's military organization. He seemed to think the troops that had attacked him in his stronghold were from another military post. Indeed, one cavalry unit from Camp Grant had attacked. The Tonto chief apparently believed the various army camps were separate armies. He assumed they were hostile to each other, as Indian bands often were. Del-che-ae sought to enlist the troops from McDowell to join him in war against the troops from Camp Grant and he offered to bring 300 more warriors to add to the 100 he had with him for an attack on Camp Grant. We can only assume the laughter this caused the garrison and the humiliation Del-che-ae must have felt at discovering how wrong he was.

In spite of the chief's misunderstanding, Commander Captain George Sanford explored with him the idea of a reservation along the Salt River. Sanford had no authority to make such an arrangement and the rations at McDowell were too low to feed this influx of Tontos. After about a week in camp, someone spread word that the Pimas were coming up from their villages to attack the Tontos so Del-che-ae and his party disappeared into the darkness.

By this time the enlistment of the Pima and Maricopa companies of Arizona Volunteers had expired. Sanford knew his soldiers could not track and surprise the Tontos without the help of Indian scouts so he requested and received authority to enlist as many as 100 of the desert Indians. The former companies of Pima and Maricopa scouts were quick to seize the opportunity and became attached to the regular troops at Fort McDowell. They wore the red flannel bands on their heads to distinguish them and these head bands quickly became the proud symbol of the Indian scouts. Their chiefs, Azul of the Pimas and Chivaria of the Maricopas, were poised and eager for action against the Tontos. They were given a guarantee that they could do it in their own manner and on their own time while they continued to live in their villages.

Near the end of October an army expedition set out to seek the site for an outpost in Tonto territory. They followed the now familiar route over the mountains and into the Tonto Basin where they picked up an Apache trail. It led them to a rancheria deep in the Sierra Ancha, probably on Spring Creek. The ensuing attack netted six Tontos killed, five prisoners and two horses. Captain Sanford reported that this was a large and permanent village in an almost inaccessible canyon, "with a very large amount of winter stores... Among the articles found were two tin canteens, such as are issued by government, a portion of an English copy of the New Testament, some mail straps and pieces of a saddle, a gun lock and brass plates belonging to a gun, and baskets such as are used for carrying grain etc, in great numbers. They had a great abundance of seeds, nuts, acorns, buckskins, serapes, and other articles used by the Indians, and the destruction of these just as winter is setting in will be a great blow to them."

Chapter Twenty-Six

THE FIGHT ON SPRING CREEK

As the U.S. Army continued their inroads into the Tonto stronghold, seeking a location for a new post, it was evident to the Apaches they could no longer be safe by retreating to secluded fortresses. Delshay and other headmen came periodically to parlay with the white military leaders who offered them a reservation at Fort Goodwin, to the east on the Salt River. However, not only did the Tontos see this as imprisonment, there were often bad feelings with the Pinal and San Carlos bands that had settled at Fort Goodwin. Then the Tontos and Yavapai were offered a safe camp near Fort McDowell if they would settle peacefully. This was hardly acceptable because their sworn enemies, the Pimas, would be nearby. The Tontos now began to bargain for a reservation in their own Tonto Basin that would include rations and military protection.

As the year 1867 approached, the Tontos sorely felt the pinch of winter. So many of their stores had been destroyed and so much of their freedom to hunt had been taken away, their raids now took a desperate, wider girth. They increased the numbers of their warriors by cooperative ventures with the Yavapai and at times with the Mojave. During January and February the Indians staged a series of raids on Fort McDowell taking horses, mules, and hides for their cold and starving families.

On February 19th a military party left Camp McDowell to choose a site in the Tonto territory for an outpost to be named Camp Reno. The name was to honor Major General Jesse Lee Reno, killed in a Civil War battle in Maryland. Pima and Maricopa scouts were to have accompanied the party. They had been at McDowell drawing rations and clothing since their December enlistment. Because a new commander, outranking Sanford, had come to McDowell whom the Indians did not respect, the scouts refused to prepare for this mission. The day before the planned departure they disobeyed orders and returned to their villages on the Gila River. The Tontos, observing the smaller military party headed for their Sierra Ancha stronghold without native scouts, spread the word among their bands. They allowed the soldiers to enter a beautiful valley on Spring Creek, just south of Diamond Butte. The army had named it Meadow Valley; in later settlement days it became the location of the Flying W Ranch. Sanford's detachment had been there before and they knew several rancherias were there but these had been deserted while the army advanced. That afternoon, February 22nd, the weather turned cold and a heavy snow began to fall. The Tontos then closed the net they had planned. In a highly unusual move they attacked the soldiers' camp at two o'clock in the morning, taking the whites by surprise.

Amazingly, only one white man was killed, a packer, and a corporal was wounded, before the army could repulse the Tontos with superior firepower. When the attackers scattered, the soldiers moved their camp to the top of the hill and waited defensively until dawn. At least one hundred fifty Tontos set up ambuscades on the hills and passes, preventing escape. Other Tontos approached within two hundred yards of the troops to snipe at them from behind trees. The soldiers tried to march in first one direction and then another but the deep snow and Tonto positions had them hemmed in. The troops had to dismount and defend themselves from behind trees. Indian bullets penetrated the coat and belt of the accompanying surgeon, Dr. Charles Smart. The troops held their position until the dark of night when they escaped by detouring over the mountain. The deep snow and heavy forest made their retreat extremely difficult.

When one of the pack mules could not keep up with the march the soldiers killed it and left it behind. The starving Tontos descended upon it to feast which gave the army its opportunity to get away. The natives had won the day, not only in defeating the goal of the soldiers but also in proving again the Sierra Ancha stronghold was a most illogical place for a military post. When army headquarters continued to insist on establishing a post in the heart of Tonto territory, Fort McDowell's commander suggested a site in Tonto Basin would be more reasonable.

As the military detachment returned to Camp McDowell it was taunted all the way by Tontos who occasionally showed themselves and fired into the company. When throughout the month of March the army made no forays against them the Tontos felt some sense of victory. However, in April seventy soldiers and one hundred eighty Indian scouts moved over the trails toward the Sierra Ancha. Interestingly, many of the Pimas and Maricopas refused to cooperate with their white commanders and lit large campfires that warned of their approach. By the time the army company again reached the valleys of the Sierra Ancha the rancherias had been abandoned.

Chapter 27

The Road Into The Heartland

The U. S. Army was learning the hard way about the nature of Apache warfare. When General McDowell submitted his second annual report to General Halleck, Commander of the Military Division of the Pacific, September 14, 1867, he included what he had learned.

"The hostilities in (Arizona) are made by Indians who live in the mountainous parts of the Territory, where nature has combined everything to favor the life of murder and rapine they lead. They require a peculiar kind of warfare, and a peculiar force to carry it on successfully. It is not so much a large force as an active one that is needed. It is more like hunting wild animals than any kind of regular warfare. The Indians are seldom in large bodies, and never take any risk. They move with great celerity, unencumbered with any baggage, and when out on their forays can seldom be overtaken. When they are, and are pressed, they give way and disperse among the mountains and ravines, so that it is impossible to follow them... They can only be successfully fought by troops who carry on an offensive warfare against them, who do not wait till they have attacked... but who fight them in their own way: take no baggage, move by night, and hide during the day; creep upon their camps and rush upon them by surprise..."

It was still the strategy of the army to establish a military post in the heartland of the Tonto Apaches to be named Camp Reno. In a communique to the commander at Fort McDowell, General Sherburne, Adjutant of the Military Department of California, wrote, "One of the objects in seeking to establish Camp Reno was to be able to have a force far enough in the heart of Indian Country to be able to have the Indians on a reservation in the mountains where they would be away from any danger of collision with the whites or the friendly Indians."

This goal would occupy the troops out of Camp McDowell for the next eleven months. On October 10, 1867 two companies left McDowell under the command of Lt. Dubois. They had with them forty fully loaded pack mules, one wagon and a herd of beef cattle. The cattle immediately attracted the attention of the Tontos who stampeded the cattle twice in one day but failed to make off with them. The soldiers kept the Indians at bay while they followed the old trail that bordered Sycamore Creek.

Building the new trail was labor intensive with many boulders to blast, hillsides to cut and washes to bridge. A constant guard had to be kept against the Indians that lurked in the surrounding hills. This startling invasion of their stronghold was driving the various Tonto Apache bands together along with bands of Pinal Apaches and Yavapai. Even though they were not all amicable they realized their continued existence required new alliances.

The army had their own allies in the Pima and Maricopa tribes and braves from both groups enlisted as scouts. They accompanied the troops and used their free time to search out the Apaches. During October and November they succeeded in killing fifteen Apaches and taking twelve prisoners (one woman and eleven children).

On November 11th Apache signal fires on the surrounding hills indicated a desire for peace. A small group of them appeared on the edge of the soldiers' camp and shouted in Spanish that they were friendly. There followed an exchange of white truce flags, the Indians leaving theirs with the soldiers while carrying the army white flag back to their hideaway, along with some used clothes and trinkets, with a promise to return with their chief in four days. They also carried Lt. DuBois' invitation for the chief to bring his entire band in to the camp. Such an act would mean food for the Indians.

When DuBois notified his superiors of his plan with a request for an interpreter the acting commander at Camp McDowell dispatched 170 mounted Indian scouts toward the army encampment. They were under the command of Chief Azul. When they arrived they were upset to learn the soldiers had let the apaches leave the camp. Two days later three Tontos approached bearing a white flag and said that the presence of their enemies, the Pima and Maricopa scouts, precluded the Apaches from coming in for a conference. DuBois asked them to wait on a ridge near where the soldiers were working on the road and at evening he would give them safe passage to the camp.

When the Pimas learned of the Apache presence they rushed the spot waving their war clubs and rifles. The twenty-five year old DeBois, short at just five feet four inches, placed himself between the Pimas and the Tontos. Through a Spanish interpreter he told the Pimas there would be no killing in his camp. The Pimas responded with a war-cry and rushed to attack the unarmed Tontos, severely wounding two of them. DuBois did not call his small detachment to help, knowing it would precipitate a deadly skirmish. Instead he drew his revolver and held off the Pimas. At that instant DuBois' old tuberculosis erupted and his lung hemorrhaged splattering blood on his face. Those around thought he had been struck by a Pima war club. This quieted the Pimas who stood on the sidelines jeering while the two wounded Tontos and DuBois were taken back to camp in a wagon.

The next day the wounded Tontos, who had been under guard all night, were able to be up and about. Azul's scout returned to Camp McDowell to report four Apaches killed, one wounded, and one woman and eight children captured. This was a family that had been on their way to the soldiers' camp under the promise of a peaceful conference.

Chapter Twenty-Eight

ATTEMPTS AT GOOD WILL

In spite of the threat of lurking Pima Indian scouts Chief Del-che-ae entered Camp Miller with 50 men, women and children on November 22, 1867 and met with Captain DuBois. The Tonto headman professed trust in The Little Captain, as Del-che-ae called him, based on the commander's heroic action in saving the three Tontos from the Pimas. However, Del-che-ae further stated he would not honor a previous treaty in which the army offered to locate the Tontos near Camp McDowell. That location was too close to their enemies. DuBois then suggested the Tontos could settle near the site of the soon-to-be-established Camp Reno. Since this was in their own territory the chief agreed on the condition his people be given rations, clothing, blankets, tobacco, ammunition for hunting and the freedom to hunt and gather according to their custom. Dubois agreed to all except the ammunition and encouraged Del-che-ae to get his people to change their lifestyle and become farmers. That way, he assured them, they would be rich like their enemies the Pimas and Maricopas who had cooperated with the whites from the beginning.

Most of Del-che-ae's people left Camp Miller after the talk, although the chief remained until November 24th with fourteen of his warriors. He invited DuBois to come with him to his rancheria. It would be a sign of good faith on both of their parts. DuBois would show courage and a willingness to trust the Tonto and the Tonto would take him to their hidden stronghold. DuBois exhibited tremendous bravery when he took Del-che-ae up on the offer and accompanied the chief alone and unarmed. During DuBois' absence, Lt. Chilson assumed command of the road crew.

It was a rough 30 mile ride over the Mazatzals, across the Tonto Basin, and deep into the Sierra Ancha. The winds of approaching winter swept off the Mogollon Rim to the north, but DuBois was warmed by a cordial reception and blazing fires in the Apache camp. They had built a wickiup for him, with a fire in front of it, and served him a supper of mescal and tortillas. The Tontos tended to his horse while three circles of warriors gathered around his fire. The Apache council silently passed a pipe, allowing their thoughts to settle. They talked among themselves until midnight about his proposal for them to settle near Camp Reno when it was established in exchange for protection and food. DuBois strained to follow their talk using what little of their language he had picked up. He learned that three other chiefs were present, among them the Pinal Apache Ash-cav-o-til who refused to smoke the pipe with DuBois. However, after Del-che-ae told the story of DuBois risking his life to save the three Tontos, Ash-cav-o-til took up the pipe again and made his peace with the soldier. The conference concluded with handshakes and a promise by the Apaches to guarantee the safety of Americans traveling alone through their territory.

That night DuBois was guarded, for his own safety, by three warriors, two of whom he had saved from the Pimas. One or the other of them kept his leg on DuBois throughout the night, undoubtedly wanting to make sure the white man did not leave nor do any of them harm. Mutual trust was obviously not complete. The next morning, after sunrise, DuBois was escorted back to Camp Miller, arriving there late in the afternoon on November 25th.

That same day Del-che-ae returned the visit, bringing 70 of his men, women and children to Camp Miller. The warriors were armed and the majority of the Apache group camped apart from the soldiers. Eight of them were invited to remain in the military camp and sleep in the tents of the officers. Some enlisted men resented having to cook and make coffee for the Apaches. Their complaints compared this to "taking a rattlesnake into your bed," and secretly they served spoiled flour to their Indian guests. When Del-che-ae and his company returned to their stronghold, he and Ash-cav-o-til made plans to settle their bands near the army encampment. The military road had progressed slowly but was now far enough beyond Camp Miller to warrant a new base named Camp Carroll. The name honored Lt. C. C. Carroll who was recently killed by Apaches in southeast Arizona. The construction problems of the army and the hunger problems of the Apaches were compounded by the winter rains which had descended upon central Arizona. About 300 Indians began gathering near Camp Carroll and they were joined by a band of Mescalero Apaches called Zish-in-til. It is hard to imagine why they had come into Tonto Territory unless they had been fleeing white settlement in New Mexico. Each of the headmen affirmed their willingness to accept DuBois' offer of a reservation in the Tonto Basin and to seal their good faith they brought samples of free floating gold. They claimed it had come from just over the mountain near Tonto Creek. For his part DuBois arranged an exchange of two Apache prisoners held by the Pimas for two Mexican boys held by the Apaches.

Chapter Twenty-Nine

GOOD WILL ENDING

Captain DuBois sought to make good on his promises to the bands of Tonto, Pinal, and Mescalero Apaches that had encamped near Camp Carroll. He began to issue daily one pound of meat and one pound of flour with some salt to each Indian. He also requested permission from his superiors to distribute used clothing, blankets and tents. All of these arrangements exceeded his authority but DuBois knew he had to do it to buy time while the road was completed into the Tontos' homeland. He further requested that the Pima and Maricopa scouts cease their forays in the Tonto Basin.

While Del-che-ae and the others were camped there they received a visit from the newly appointed commander of all troops operating in northern and central Arizona, Col. Thomas Devin. He stayed only briefly, but did approve DuBois' plan and later secured final approval from General McDowell.

The road construction continued with little interference from the Indians and reached Sunflower Valley in the heart of the Mazatzal Mountains. There the army established a third camp and named it Camp O'Connell, honoring a major who had died in Texas the previous September. DuBois' tubercular condition caused more hemorrhages and he was transferred for medical disability on February 4, 1868. Lt. George Chilson took command of the troops building the military road and at the same time a new commander took over at Camp McDowell, Major David R. Clendenin of the 8th Cavalry. Chief Del-che-ae and the other headmen who were camped with their bands in Sunflower Valley received a visit from Clendenin the end of February. He confronted them, asking why the Apaches robbed and murdered Americans. Del-che-ae answered that Indians needed what whites possessed and raiding was the only way they had to obtain such goods. The chief further suggested that the Tontos would work hard and honestly if they had military protection and rations. He even offered to send warriors to fight with the soldiers against other Tontos who did not cooperate.

Clendenin, convinced of Del-che-ae's sincerity, promised protection and that rations would be provided. He invited the chiefs to join him in locating the site for Camp Reno and their future farms. As they prepared to ride out of camp, Del-che-ae suddenly refused to go along. It seems Major Clendenin was mounted while the Apache chief was expected to walk. This humiliation was unacceptable to the Tonto and the friendly relationship suddenly evaporated in the winter air. The Apache may have welcomed this as an excuse. Del-cha-ae did not wish to lend his full weight to a military post in the heart of Apacheria nor did he want to appear as cozying up to the white soldiers. Clendenin was angry at the rebuff and returned to Camp McDowell.

The following month, on March 24th, while the Indian bands were still camped near Camp O'Connell, another new commander from Camp McDowell arrived to parlay with the Indians. His name was Major Andrew J. Alexander. It was extremely bewildering to the Indians to have such frequent changes of command. They no sooner became familiar with the personality of one when he was replaced by a stranger. Major Alexander was not just on a social visit but was in pursuit of Apache raiders who had allegedly killed two herdsmen near Picacho Peak and driven 700 head of cattle in the direction of Tonto territory. A cavalry unit followed him over the mountain.

Alexander's talks with the Indians had to go through a double translation, Apache translated into Spanish and then the Spanish into English. By the time answers went through the same process misunderstandings readily occurred. The officer did make it clear he wanted the Apaches to remain camped in Sunflower Valley until he returned from his search for the stolen cattle. The Indians seemed to agree until suddenly the cavalry unit from Camp McDowell appeared over the hill. As they began their ominous looking descent into the valley one of the chiefs rallied his people and they disappeared into the mountains. Del-che-ae lingered but as the cavalry set up camp he and his people melted into the surrounding juniper and oak covered canyons.

It was April 3rd when the cavalry detachment continued their search for the stolen cattle. They rode up into the Sierra Ancha not realizing they were riding directly into Del-che-ae's stronghold. Suddenly a line of Apaches blocked the trail before them as they crested a hill. Standing defiantly on a rock silhouetted against the sky was Del-cha-ae. He held a rifle, wore an army blouse and a black hat. He shouted that he had come out to meet the "Capitan Grande," a name he had for the commander and to declare war against the Americans. He said he had made up his mind the night before that blood was required and the general should take his army and leave the country. Furthermore, he said, one of the chieftains was leading an army of a thousand warriors to attack the army camp and wipe them out.

As the chief spoke he gesticulated wildly and broke into abusive language. With that, Major Alexander ordered his men to shoot the chief. One of the soldiers who corresponded regularly with Prescott's *Arizona Miner* under the pen name "Reno," wrote, "The words were not finished when about half a dozen bullets greeted the chief, leaving nothing to be seen of him but his breechclout, the Apache national flag, floating for an instant, and then disappearing. The infantry and cavalry ascended the hill immediately, but the Indians were nowhere to be found..."

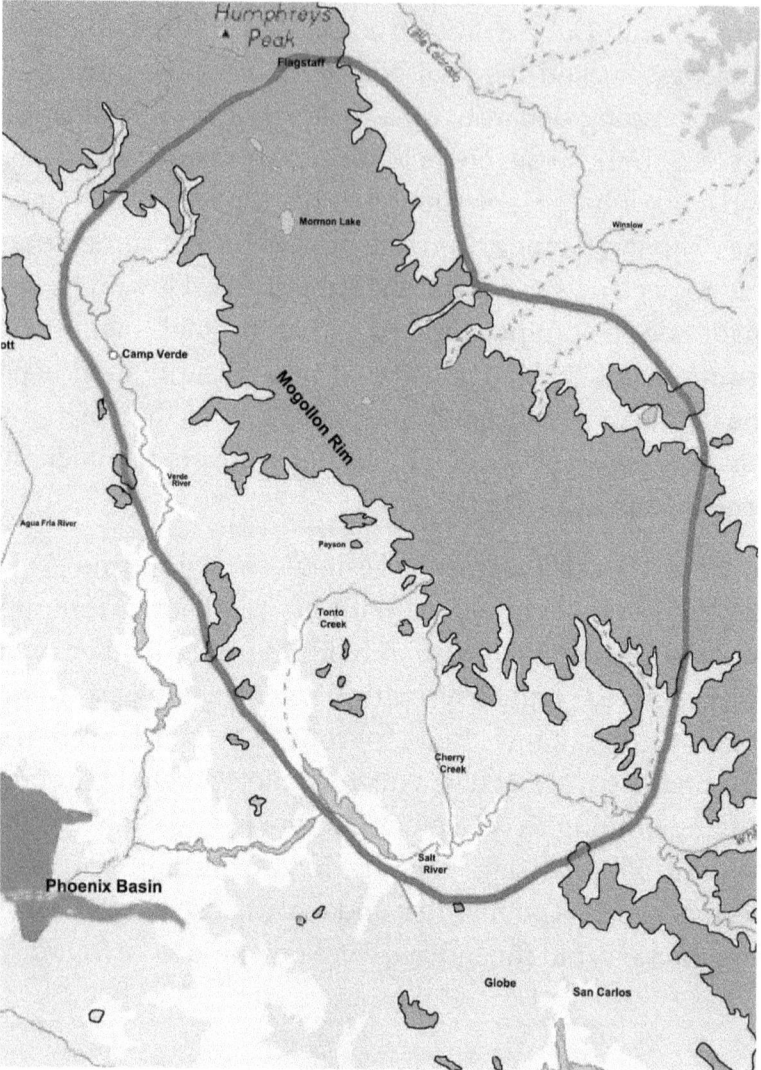

The extent of the Tonto Apache
homeland before settlers arrived.

Bedrock metates with North Peak
in the background.

An Apache woman with water jug.
Sketch by Donn Morris

Apache gowas.

Apache women and child in front of a gowa.

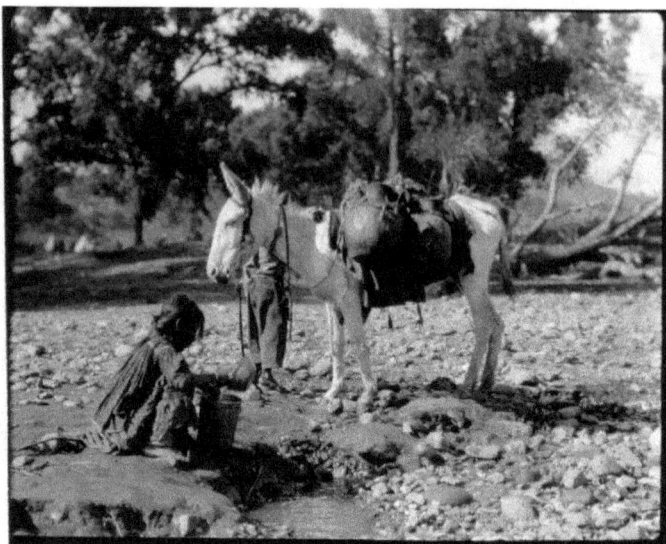

An Apache woman getting water
with a burro.

Camp Apache, 1873.

GENERAL GEORGE CROOK ON THE TRAIL.

Troops before the Battle of
Big Dry Wash, July 17, 1882.

Indian Scouts at Camp Verde, c 1870's.

The Guard House at San Carlos
Reservation, 1880.

Tonto Apache man, c. 1894.

San Carlos Reservation trade token.

Apache workers at Roosevelt, c. 1909.

Henry Evans, Tonto Apache scout.

King S. Woolsey

Crown Dancers, 2014.

Apache burden basket.

Tonto Apache beaded belt, c. 1960's.

Beaded necklace made by
Jerri DeCola Johnson.

"Pitch Pot" made by Rhea Delma.

Chapter Thirty

MIXED SIGNALS FROM THE TONTOS

In early April 1868, Chief Del-che-ae shouted a declaration of war as the army invaded his stronghold in the Sierra Ancha. The troops boldly continued their march toward Meadow Valley (Spring Creek) looking for stolen cattle. The Tontos hid themselves until one of the army units began climbing out of that deep valley. The Apaches set an ambush and a fifteen-minute skirmish followed. The troops dislodged the Indians and retreated without further incident.

It became obvious to the military that an outpost in the Sierra Ancha was impractical. It would be impossible to keep a supply line through such rugged terrain where the Tontos were so deeply ensconced. Still the army was under orders to establish a post deeper into Del-che-ae's stronghold.

The road building crew camped on Reno Creek three miles west of Tonto Creek along an arroyo coming from Mount Ord. This was to have been the last camp along the road over the Mazatzals to a military post deep in Tonto territory. The Apaches observed cattle and supplies being moved to the new camp and did their best to harass the soldiers. This was getting too close to lands they held sacred.

On April 20, 1868 a detachment of troops forged a trail up Tonto Basin following Wild Rye Creek and around Snowstorm Mountain into a place they named Green Valley. It would one day become the location of Payson, Arizona. Here they considered a possible location for the permanent Camp Reno. An army correspondent, under the pen name of Reno, wrote to Prescott's *Arizona Miner*, "This valley is... a splendid place for a post and to hunt Indians... With plenty of cavalry the Apache will be kept hopping. Let the posts be planted in the homes of the reptiles at any expense, a road made there and it is the end of the hostile Apache in Arizona." As they returned from Green Valley the detachment killed ten Tontos.

On May 24, 1868 Del-cha-ae made an appearance once again. He claimed to have received six bullet wounds from the confrontation with Major Alexander's troops the previous month. Obviously, they healed because he led 150 warriors in an attack on the herd at the camp on Reno Creek. His encounters with the army convinced him that the white military was not to be trusted and from that decisive hour he did not hesitate to deal with them as enemies. Sometimes he would compromise in order to win food for his people, appearing at the army camps and pretending to negotiate in peace. Such efforts were always short-lived. His on-again, off-again professions of peace earned Del-che-ae the moniker "the liar."

On the other hand, one of the Pinal Apache chiefs, Ash-cav-o-til, became convinced the only way to save his people was to cooperate with the growing white presence.

He was soon disillusioned. Four men of his band entered the army camp under a flag of truce. They were bringing a message from their chief, apologizing for the time they ran away when the cavalry rode into camp. Now they wished to return. However, the four messengers were thrown into prison. Several Yavapais as well as three men and seven women and children from Del-cha-ae's band were also placed in the guardhouse. The soldiers raped two of the Tonto women. One of the men escaped and yelled curses at the Americans from a nearby hill. Another was shot and killed trying to escape.

While Del-cha-ae and Ash-cav-o-til cooperated with each other against the military when it suited a mutual purpose, they did not hesitate to play each other off for their own benefit. Ash-cav-o-til complained to the army that his band had been unjustly blamed for raids made by the Tontos. He offered to fight the Tontos and to furnish hay and wood to the soldiers as well as make adobe bricks for the proposed buildings at Camp Reno. He would then expect seed for planting and the tools used in building the road after it was finished. The growing desperation of the Indians was evident in their willingness to sell each other out in exchange for the good offices of the Army. Thus the Tontos found themselves fighting not only white men but rival bands over the hunting and planting grounds.

Chapter Thirty-One

INVASION FROM THE NORTH

In the spring of 1868 construction on the military road resumed with a plan to develop it all the way to Green Valley. Throughout the month of May the Apaches and Yavapai kept watch on the movements of a large detachment from Camp Lincoln led by Col. Thomas Devin. The line of 60 pack mules obviously meant a lengthy scout and though the Indians were not privy to Devin's plan, it was gleefully announced in Prescott's *Arizona Miner*, April 25, 1868.

> "It is the design of (Brevet) General Devin to scour the country east of the Verde, between the Mogollon range of mountains and Salt River, and if possible corral the redskins and bring them to law. To accomplish this, we learn that simultaneously troops will start out from Camps Lincoln and McDowell, on the Rio Verde, Camp Goodwin on the Gila, Camp Grant on the San Pedro, and Camp Reno in Tonto Basin. The General took with him from the post at Prescott, Fort Whipple, two companies... From Camp Lincoln the General will... take all the men that can be spared from... that post. Competent guides will accompany the expedition, and we earnestly hope that success may crown the efforts of the `boys in blue' to cripple and destroy the red thieves and murderers of Tonto Basin..."

The Tontos made sure Devin's expedition fell far short of its desired effect. The companies of cavalry and infantry followed the Clear Creek trail out of the Verde Valley and over the Mogollon Rim. At the headwaters of the East Verde River they made a switch-back trail down the nearly perpendicular cliff, which Devin called "the jump off."

While camped during the making of the switch back trail, the troops were fired upon by Tonto Apaches, killing one horse. The detachment continued exploring the side canyons to the left and right and found a number of freshly abandoned rancherias. Following Indian trails to the east, probably along the later Highline Trail that would connect homesteads under the Mogollon Rim, the soldiers reached Tonto Creek and found a series of Apache farms. The Indians hurriedly left in the midst of planting their summer crops. At this point, Devin realized his supplies would not allow him to go so far as San Carlos, his intended goal. In his June 12, 1868 report he stated, "Before starting, I had assumed that the pack animals would carry 250 pounds anywhere the cavalry could go. This I found to be an error as they could not average 200 pounds, and with that could not make over 10 miles a day in a mountain country. In endeavoring to accomplish even that, several gave out, others were killed falling over precipices and some of the rations were lost."

Col. Devin set up a camp at the head of Tonto Creek and sent his pack train back to Camp Lincoln to get 20 more days of rations during which time he scouted through the Tonto Basin without encountering the skittish Tontos. However, as the pack train retraced the route it was attacked by Tontos at the top of the Jump Off. Apache arrows killed the chief packer, a civilian named John C. Baker. The other packers held off the attackers while the cavalry escort, lagging behind, raced up the steep grade to the scene. They chased off the Tontos with their rifle fire and buried Mr. Baker's body in the rocky ground. They then obscured the grave's location with their horses' hoof prints so the Tontos would not disinter the body for mutilation. As they proceeded westward they passed the highest point on the Mogollon Rim, a forested volcanic cone, which they named Baker's Butte to honor their fallen comrade.

With renewed supplies the Devin detachment continued eastward through Tonto Territory without any skirmishes. On their return trip the Tontos were still nowhere to be seen and Devin jumped to an interesting but wrong conclusion. He reported, "The Tonto Basin has heretofore been property supposed to be the home of the Apaches, where they had farms, families and stock. It has probably contained a large population, as we found rancherias sufficient for hundreds of families, but all abandoned... The Indians have (with the exception of a few predatory bands) either left the country west of the San Carlos, or have sent their families beyond..."

The Devin expedition served to further increase the thirst of white settlers for Tonto lands. Members of his party elaborated on what they saw in the *Arizona Miner*, June, 1868,

> "The most attractive, best watered and richest agricultural section of this Territory lies east of the Verde. In the Tonto Basin, north and east of the Sierra Anchas, streams of delicious water were found at intervals of from three to five miles. Springs were plenty, and one, the largest ever seen by any of the party, was estimated to have a flow of several hundred gallons per minute. The basin of the spring holds eight hundred gallons, and the whole surface was in commotion. It supplies the greater part of the main branch of the east fork of the Verde..."

The reporter was probably describing the copious spring that still flows in Whispering Pines on the site of the old John Meadows ranch.

Chapter Thirty-Two
ATTACKS ON CAMP RENO

When the army commanders decided an outpost in Green Valley would stretch their supply line too far, they established the post on Reno Wash as a more permanent location. The army's cattle herd was moved to Camp Reno and immediately Del-che-ae led 150 warriors, only a few of whom were mounted, on a raid. The herd was stampeded during a hand-to-hand skirmish between Indians and the military herders but Del-che-ae's group was routed as soon as the alerted cavalry troops arrived. Three Indians were killed, eight wounded, and the brother of Del-che-ae was taken prisoner. What happened next was reported by Reno in the June 13, 1868, *Arizona Miner*.

"(On May 24th) the chief's brother, who was one of our prisoners and the best looking Indian in the tribe, attempted to make his escape and was shot dead by the guard. The remainder of the prisoners are rather inclined to remain. Chief Del-che-ae's brother was named `Rising Sun' and was thought more of by the tribe than any other Indian. He had been cautioned against trying to escape, but said he was bound to go and, if killed, his bones would neither make silver nor gold. So the `Rising Sun' of the tribe is set."

If ever Del-che-ae resolved for an all-out war with the white invaders it was now. During the rest of 1868 Del-che-ae's band was being blamed for attacks on wagon trains from Tucson to LaPaz, far more activity than would have been humanly possible for his single group. However, Del-che-ae's warriors did attack the mail trains plying between McDowell and Reno. These were usually small military detachments, vulnerable as they rode along the steep mountain sides and deep ravines of the Reno Road. Apaches were after the army mules which they relished for food and furthermore the mail trains often carried the soldiers' pay. While the greenbacks were worthless to the Indians, confiscating the money created hardship and morale problems for their enemy. An especially bloody raid on the mail party occurred in the middle of June at Toddy Mountain along the Reno Road. Today the location is called Black Mountain. The remains of four soldiers were taken to the post cemetery at Camp McDowell for burial. During this period the defending army killed dozens of Tonto warriors.

The supply line to McDowell was too extended to support very many troops. As the summer wore on the garrison got down to as few as 23, an officer being rotated with the troops every 30 days. Perhaps the low number of soldiers encouraged a number of peaceful Apaches from other Tonto, Pinal and Yavapai families to settle near Camp Reno. They worked crops along the Tonto Creek bottomland and sold hay cut from the abundant grasses to the post. It was difficult for the soldiers to know at any given moment who were the peaceful Indians and who were enemies. Individuals came and went, keeping the army guessing.

The berry harvest was plentiful along the streams in the summer of 1868 and proved some small relief to the hungry Tontos who still held out in the mountains. Desperate for meat, they continued attacks against the army livestock during July. Early in the month Del-che-ae's band descended upon a government herd en route to Camp Reno and made off with a dozen of the animals. The cavalry pursued them into the Sierra Ancha where the trail of the animals was lost. The soldiers did come upon a camp of 70 or 80 Tontos who, with the first shot, escaped in all directions. Later that month, Del-che-ae's warriors teamed up with those of Escavotil, the Pinal Apache, and Wah-poo-eta, a Yavapai, to attack the herd again at Camp Reno. The almost 200 warriors were driven off by twenty soldiers from McDowell who arrived to take up positions at the outpost.

On July 20th, a major thunderstorm hit the post and during its hour-long duration the Indian prisoners escaped from the newly constructed stockade. Ten days later, the Tontos went after the herd again but soldiers drove the livestock into the stockade before any were stolen. Hunger continued to gnaw at the morale of the Tontos and while they grew more desperate in their raids many wanted to compromise with the white man. The Cherry Creek band of Tontos led by chief Osh-kol-te came into Camp Reno making peace signs, but the officer in charge rebuffed them.

On the evening of November 30, 1868 a meteorite shot across the Tonto Basin in a golden shower and crashed over the horizon with a rumbling like thunder and a shockwave like a small earthquake. The night lit up as day. The soldiers wondered if this had been a sign for change to the Tontos because during the next several months a strange peace descended over the Rim Country. However, this may have been due less to the heavenly sign than to the fact that Del-che-ae was busy obtaining a supply of guns and ammunition from the Navajos and the Hopis in the north.

Chapter Thirty-Three

PEACE FOR FOOD

As the winter of 1869 progressed desperate hunger among the Apaches and Yavapai led to an outburst of raids and killings throughout the territory. The military command began to question whether the war was worth the $3,000,000 cost each year. There was even speculation that these Indian territories were not ready for occupation. If the Tonto bands could have listened in on such conversations, they would have been heartened. However, the government reached the conclusion that since there was so much white settlement on all sides of Tonto territory the military had to stay. After all, this government expenditure provided Arizona's primary economic base and if it was withdrawn many of the settlers who made a living supplying the army would have to quit the territory. As often happens in war, economic advantages continued the slaughter.

The alternative to the white settlers' failed efforts at genocide seemed to be a system of reservations. Feeding the Indians would cost less than war. An investigating group reported that if a reservation were large enough to afford plenty of hunting and gathering in addition to farming and supplemental rations it might work.

At the same time cooperation between Apache and Yavapai bands was increasing, creating larger raiding parties on the white settlements. The Indians perceived that the troops from Camp McDowell were in a weakened condition. The horses were worn out, personnel were shorthanded and the soldiers were occupied with escort services for supply trains and mail carriers. It was a good time for the natives to negotiate some sort of peace. The Indian chiefs were told they would have to surrender unconditionally in exchange for the protection of a reservation and rations. Del-che-ae insisted on a clarification. Exactly what lands would be set aside for them? They could not answer this and at the same time the soldiers were harassing the Tonto encampment at Reno so Del-che-ae took his people and left.

During the next months the Indian bands and military commanders played a game of tag. Neither side trusted the other, nor did the Indian bands trust each other. Headmen would bring their people into Camp Reno or Camp McDowell for conferences, only to leave again at the slightest provocation. At one point Del-che-ae and the others encamped less than a mile from the Reno stockade and the Apache warriors traded bows and arrows with the soldiers for bread and tobacco. Two of the Tonto chiefs, Del-che-ae and Skit-la-no-yah, responded to an invitation to go to Camp McDowell to negotiate the peace. The terms they were given stated that there would be no handouts of food until the Indians surrendered unconditionally, or as an alternative they agreed to be army scouts. Those who signed up as scouts would have their families held hostage at Camp Reno as a guarantee. All Apaches desiring peace would go to Camp McDowell where a reservation would be established across the Verde River from the post. There they would be given protection, food and used clothing. All who did not conform would be considered hostile and liable to be killed on sight. No Indians would be allowed near Camp Reno, so close to their stronghold. The chiefs were given 60 days to accept these terms after which they would be considered hostiles.

It was near the end of March when the Apache chiefs returned to Camp Reno and presented the terms to their bands. All rejected such an agreement. March turned to April and Osh-kol-ti, the Tonto chief whose people ranged from Cherry Creek to the Four Peaks, joined the others at Camp Reno asking for food. The command at Reno had changed again, with Lt. George Chilson in charge. He met with Del-che-ae, Cha-li-pun, and Skit-la-vis-yah to discuss the surrender terms again under friendly skies. Chilson knew the Indians well enough to realize any agreement on their part to the conditions was not to be thought of as final. Peace for the Tonto and Yavapai bands was only a respite between hostilities, a time to rest and recuperate, a time to be fed and protected from their enemies.

The chiefs were not prepared to move their people to McDowell until after the corn harvest in the fall. Chilson was able to secure agreement to this from his superiors, postponing the 60 day time limit for agreement to the terms of peace. Chilson sought to maintain his own truce with the Indians, trading their maintenance tasks around the post for leftovers out of the kitchen. A further financial arrangement was made whereby the Indians would transport the mail between Reno and McDowell in a one-day courier service each way and be paid $25.00 a month in gold coin along with rations.

Chapter Thirty-Four

APACHES TURN ON EACH OTHER

Lt. Chilson, the officer in charge of Camp Reno, had enough good will among the Apaches that he was able to have long conversations with Del-che-ae. The Tonto chief gave Chilson detailed descriptions of Indian politics, including current friction between the Tonto bands and the Pinal band of Ash-cav-o-til, as well as with the Yavapai bands of Osh-kol-te and Wa-poo-eta. The Yavapai bands joined together for raids against Tucson and as far west as the mine camps around Wickenburg, but the Tontos were often blamed and were resentful. Del-che-ae "also told me," wrote Chilson to Lt. Kane, post adjutant at McDowell, "many other things about the localities they frequent and in what places they are most always to be found, and his story agrees as well with my own knowledge and ideas of the country, that it is impossible for me to discredit his statement." Del-che-ae also confided some startling news. It seemed that even though Osh-kol-te had professed peace, he was actually planning a major raid on the Wickenburg area, along with his Yavapai cohorts. They were storing food in the Sunflower area where their women and children were camped to keep an eye on military movements in and out of Reno. Osh-kol-te threatened Del-che-ae's life if he revealed these things but Del-che-ae believed his best interest was to side with the U.S. Army. He gave Chilson detailed information about the trails the raiders were to take and Chilson notified the army at McDowell. An Apache courier from McDowell responded the next day that the army was preparing a venture with cavalry and Maricopa scouts to ascend the Verde and head off the projected raid.

Suddenly, on April 23rd Osh-kol-te arrived at Camp Reno and joined the discussions between Del-che-ae and Chilson. It was the first opportunity Chilson had to explain to the Yavapai chief the peace plan requiring the unconditional surrender. Osh-kol-te said he would do whatever Del-che-ae did about it. Chilson did not believe him in light of Del-che-ae's earlier information. Three days later two scouting parties set out from McDowell to head off the Yavapai raiders. One detachment went up the Verde River with two companies of cavalry and the Maricopa scouts while a second made up of Pima scouts went twenty miles up the Verde from the post and then cut over the Mazatzals. These actions were observed by Yavapai lookouts and Osh-kol-te's group remained at Reno abandoning their plans for Wickenburg.

The first week of May Chilson prepared a census of the various bands camped in the Reno vicinity. Del-che-ae emerged as the most influential among the chiefs, less than 30 years of age, headman for a band of 100 warriors, 40 women and 60 children. Fifteen or twenty of his warriors carried firearms, from single barreled shotguns to improved Spencer breech-loaders. Their penchant for gambling meant the weapons frequently exchanged owners.

Chilson's census showed that the Tonto and Yavapai men, women and children outnumbered the soldiers five to one. More significantly, there were two warriors for every available soldier and the two sides had equal firepower. While this information was gathered, an infantryman shot and wounded one of Osh-kol-te's warriors, precipitating the mass exodus of that band from Camp Reno.

Significant events were taking place in Arizona Territory with the appointment of Anson Safford as the new governor. He disagreed with the long held government policy of extermination for the Indians and wanted instead to spend more money on reservations. After studying Chilson's report the military commanders decided the more reasonable attitudes were expressed by the governor and others. It was time to extend another peace feeler to Del-che-ae and the other chiefs. Mules would be sent to them for their transportation to McDowell. Before this could be put into effect a lieutenant came from Washington to inspect the military posts of McDowell, Reno and Lincoln. The commander of the Military District of Arizona, Major Alexander, accompanied the inspector on the tour. The *Arizona Miner* of May 29, 1869, quoted Alexander affirming his trust in Del-che-ae's sincerity. He reported that the Indians faithfully carried the mail, harvested hay, served as scouts, and that Del-che-ae said his people were weary of war; that they would ally with the U.S. Army and help to fight hostile Indians.

Alexander then traveled to San Francisco carrying his public relations effort to the Department of the Pacific. He hoped to secure permission for a reservation near Camp Reno. While he was gone, troops from Camp McDowell continued to pursue Apache and Yavapai bands, destroying their villages and crops and taking many prisoners. One of the camps turned out to be the stronghold of Pinal Apache chief Ash-cav-o-til. He had been utilizing an ancient pueblo with its large cultivated areas, irrigation ditches, and ball courts. Among the artifacts recovered were U.S. Government uniforms, mail bags, blankets, soap, and Spencer carbine ammunition. Back at Camp Reno a medicine coat was identified by Chilson, Del-che-ae and Osh-kol-te as belonging to Ash-cav-o-til.

Chapter Thirty-Five

EXTERMINATION AN IMPOSSIBLE GOAL

Major Alexander returned from his trip to San Francisco seeking permission to establish a reservation and immediately his enthusiasm for Del-che-ae cooled. The chief's mail couriers were accused of kidnapping an Apache servant girl in Alexander's household at Camp McDowell. The couriers were put in the guardhouse at Camp Reno and Del-che-ae was confronted. It was discovered that Osh-cav-o-til not Del-che-ae was responsible for harboring the servant girl. In fact she was not kidnapped at all but had run away from the severe demands of Mrs. Alexander. With the help of Del-cha-ae, Chilson arranged to have the girl returned and personally delivered her to the Alexanders the first week in June 1869.

In the midst of the summer there was another leadership change at Camp Reno and again the Tontos suffered confusion. In the Apache culture chiefs acted quite independently of one another. Del-che-ae and the other chiefs never quite comprehended the complex organization that lay behind the U.S. Army and its various commands. They could relate to some officers who won their respect but not with others whom they did not trust. Chilson had earned their respect but late in July he left Reno for duty elsewhere. Arriving to take Chilson's place was a 35 year old Irishman named Captain Patrick Collins.

He would command the post until Camp Reno was abandoned a year later.

Almost immediately, an incident occurred that got Collins and Del-che-ae off to a bad start. The arrangement Chilson made with Del-che-ae and his men to carry the mail was still in effect in spite of weakening trust between the chief and the military. With the beginning of the new command at Reno, a small raiding party waylaid the mail couriers and destroyed the mail, apparently without a battle. The same party proceeded to attack the herd at Reno and steal some cattle, killing a herder. Collins thought he had reason to believe Del-che-ae and his couriers were in league with the robbers and he fired them from the lucrative job.

The summer now plunged into a new escalation of Indian raids, calls from the white community for extermination of all Indians and attempts of the tribes to bargain with the army. The various headmen would bring their groups in to Camp Reno and set up camp only to be frightened off by random shootings or an increase in military presence.

The commander of Camp Goodwin on the Gila River, Col. Green, was ordered by General Devin, commander of Arizona's Southern Military District, "to take all his available force and personally head a campaign of extermination against the Apaches in the mountains north of the Gila River."

Green took four companies of cavalry and some friendly White Mountain Apaches, under Chief Manuel, into the White Mountains where they camped at the junction of the east and west forks of the White River. On this tour they encountered and killed many Apaches, destroying crops and stock. "At this point," wrote Government Scout A.F. Banta, "Col. Green, finding himself in the very heart of Apacheria, decided to establish a camp as a working base, and name it Camp Ord." Later this location was officially approved and eventually became Fort Apache. With a road forged to it from the south the Tonto Apaches were now hemmed in on three sides. Camp Lincoln on the west, Camp McDowell on the south and Camp Ord on the east formed a pincers from which the cavalry would be able to quickly converge on the Tontos.

It was becoming clear to the military that extermination of the Indians was impossible and the game of cat and mouse was increasingly costly. Though outnumbered, the Apaches and Yavapai practiced a guerrilla warfare that white armies could never beat, except by starving them. The Tontos were even more frustrated, wanting to live amicably with the whites if only they could be given the land to continue their traditional way of life. The two cultures were completely incompatible. The Indians blended with nature and the European-Americans exploited nature. The white settlers coveted the minerals and grasses of Tonto territories and this would never make for peace. Something had to give.

For the moment, Indian attacks on ranches and government herds escalated and more Indian families were decimated before something happened to move both sides out of the quagmire.

.

Chapter Thirty-Six

CONFLICTING VIEWS OF THE ENEMY

As word went out across Arizona about the ranching and prospecting possibilities in the central mountains and basins, pressure increased on the government to provide protection for settlers. This renewed determination of the whites to take over Apache territory was reflected in the report Brevet Major General Ord made to Major General George H. Thomas, commander of the Department of the Pacific at San Francisco, dated September 27, 1869. A year and a half earlier Ord had succeeded General McDowell as Commander of the Department of California and still did not know the boundaries of the Arizona District from his comfortable and distant location in San Francisco.

He claimed success "in reducing the hostile Apaches," and went on to say, "These Arabs of Arizona have heretofore neither given nor asked quarter; their hands have always been bloody, their favorite pursuit killing and plundering, their favorite ornaments the fingers and toenails, the teeth, hair and small bones of their victims... On taking command of the department I was satisfied that the few settlers and scattered miners of Arizona were the sheep upon which these wolves habitually preyed, and that, if that wilderness was to be kept free from Apache robbers and murderers, a temporizing policy would not answer; therefore I encouraged the troops to capture and root out the Apache by every means, and to hunt them as they would wild animals."

It is interesting to compare General Ord's view of the Apaches with Army scout A. F. Banta's evaluation, regarding who were the real savages. After years of living among the Apaches of central Arizona Banta wrote, "Webster truthfully defines the so-called American savage when he says: `The savages of America, when uncorrupted by the vices of the civilized man, are remarkable for their hospitality to strangers, and for their truth, fidelity, and gratitude to their friends, but implacably cruel and revengeful toward their enemies.' But in this matter of cruelty and savagery, the civilized Christian man, with his inquisitional instruments of torture, and his witch tortures and burnings, and other methods of cruelty, is so far ahead of the so-called savage in devilishness, that he can give the red man cards and spades in the game, and then win out, thumbs down. This is a bitter pill for the `civilized' egotist to swallow; nevertheless it is the gospel truth, and cannot be truthfully contradicted."

During October and November attacks on the government herd at Reno continued. The Tontos faced a winter that could bring starvation since the army scouting parties consistently destroyed their stores of foods. Then an especially tempting opportunity presented itself. During the first week of October the army moved a large herd from the lower valley around Camp McDowell where the grass had dried up to the fine grazing around Camp Reno. On October 10th, the Tontos tried to stampede the herd, wounding a cavalry horse and killing the chief herder in the process. In these raids on livestock the Apaches sought to drive as many head as they could into the mountains. There they would feast and then drive the excess animals into canyons to become feral. There the Apaches could hunt and kill them as needed. Such cattle or mules were easier to hunt down than deer or elk.

During the first week of November what was left of the government herd was returned to Camp McDowell. An anxious peace ensued while Del-che-ae and several other chiefs petitioned under a flag of truce to occupy their former camp near Camp Reno. Captain Collins, commander at Reno, agreed until he could receive further instructions. However, he held three of Del-che-ae's warriors hostage to ensure the chief's accountability.

In the interest of fast mail service and the need for more personnel, Captain Collins again hired Del-cha-ae's Tontos to carry the mail between Camps McDowell and Reno. Construction continued on buildings at Camp Reno but any plans to extend the line of supply and build a post in Green Valley had been given up. There simply were not enough soldiers to do the job.

As 1870 dawned a crisis erupted once again. On New Year's Day Del-che-ae and several of his men left their camp on Tonto Creek for the post to visit some of the officers. The chief was unaware that the post surgeon,

James Dunlevy, believed the chief had been stealing personal items from his tent. Del-che-ae approached the surgeon's tent and upon lifting the flap was greeted by a shot from the doctor's pistol. The Tonto chief clutched his chest, turned and walked slowly through the post. As soon as he was beyond the line he gave several rallying yells and with his entire band fled to the mountains.

Apparently the wound was not serious because in a few days he returned and bragged that this was nothing! After all, Captain Alexander had earlier shot him thirty times! Del-che-ae's reference was to the time he had first openly declared war on the whites and fled amid a hail of bullets from Alexander's troops.

Chapter Thirty-Seven

THE END OF CAMP RENO

In the early months of 1870 attacks on supply trains south of the Tonto territory grew fiercer. Pinal Apaches, Yavapai, and perhaps some marauding bands of Tontos carried them out. The understaffed military posts were hardly a match for guerilla attacks that struck without warning; the Apaches had learned that a war of terror worked best. While pretending to be friendly at Camp Reno, members of Del-che-ae's bands often harbored and fed the hostile Indians and aided the Yavapai in their raids. Different bands staged surprise attacks in different sections, thus catching the army off guard, and carried out stealthy murders of lone sentinels and herders.

An evaluation of Camp Reno now took place. It was conducted by the acting assistant inspector general Lt. Col. George W. Wallace. In anticipation, Reno Commander Captain Collins placed under arrest on February 13th those Tonto bands camped at Reno. The troops hoped to keep them under guard and at peace during the visit which commenced with the lieutenant's arrival on February 17th.

Camp Reno had grown sizably with its sutler's store, Apache interpreter, blacksmith, carpenter, teamsters, clerks, herders and other civilians under contract with the army. A report of the shooting of Del-che-ae by Dr. Dunlevy reached the inspector but he chose to overlook it. He was impressed with the buildings, the stables, and the post garden cultivated about two miles away. The medical facilities left much to be desired but Reno had become a thriving community.

However, Wallace apparently made up his mind before he arrived to recommend that the post be abandoned. The road was extremely rocky and rough and the location so isolated as to make its support very costly to the government. In response to Wallace's report, the decision reached by the commanders was that Camp Reno would no longer be an independent post but become an outpost of Camp McDowell. On March 7th, Captain Collins and half the garrison returned to Camp McDowell leaving Lt. Thomas Riley and 30 troops to maintain the outpost. These remaining troops commenced building a stockade around the buildings and Camp Reno began to resemble a fort.

Seldom were the military posts in Arizona fortified in a way to be legitimately called forts. The strategy of the Apaches did not lend itself to open attack on these well-staffed military commands so there was really no need for fortifications. Before 1866, most posts in Arizona were called forts but in November of that year the Military Department of California, of which Arizona was part, directed that all Arizona posts be designated as camps, except for Whipple and Yuma. That rule was reversed in April of 1879 changing the term from camp to fort.

Deadly skirmishes continued during the spring of 1870 with bands of Apaches still considered renegades by the whites. For example, two days after the reduction of troops at Reno the paymaster's escort was attacked in Sunflower Valley while returning to Camp McDowell. Two soldiers died from that attack and several more were wounded. Four Apaches were killed.

In the middle of May a detachment of soldiers from Camp Goodwin on the Gila River established Camp Ord at the junction of the east and west forks of the White River. It was in the midst of White Mountain Apache territory and would later be named Camp Apache. Chiefs Miguel, Pedro, Petone, and Alchesay decided that the survival of their people depended on cooperating with the whites and welcomed the outpost. Its first garrison included 148 men and several civilian employees. The White Mountain Apaches were facing such impending starvation that by July 1st one thousand of them were present at Camp Ord to be counted and receive an issue of beef. More were coming in daily.

While this was going on, the Tontos continued venting their anger toward the military for using Camp Reno as a staging area against them. On June 2nd they set fire to the haystack and the wooden buildings, burning down most of the structures. After that the location continued only as a camp for the movement of troops into Apache lands. Just getting there over the Mazatzal Mountains on the Reno Road proved hazardous and the

Apache-Yavapai bands had plenty of warning by observing the troop movements.

During these same months significant changes were taking place in the military command. Arizona was separated from Southern California and made a separate military department. General George Stoneman was placed in command of both Arizona and Southern California and to the consternation of the settlers and military posts Stoneman moved the Arizona headquarters from Ft. Whipple to a place called Drum Barracks in Wilmington, California. One of his first orders was that roads be built to connect the widely separated posts throughout Arizona.

Chapter Thirty-Eight

THE U. S. SEEKS PEACE

Early in March 1870 the army introduced someone into the Arizona scene who would not only come to know the Tonto Apaches well but play a large role in diminishing their tribe. He was 23 year old Lt. John G. Bourke who came from New Mexico to Camp Grant with the 3rd Cavalry, Company F, under the command of Lt. Howard B. Cushing. Although he had just graduated from the military academy the year before, Bourke was a scholar who studied the Apaches with a scientific eye and wrote much about them and their life ways. His book, *On The Border With Crook,* is one of the finer sources of information regarding the Tonto war.

On March 19th, Commander Cushing's company, with John Bourke second in command, scouted over the Pinal Mountains, down Pinal Creek, past Wheatfields to the Salt River and Tonto Creek. They went a short way up Tonto Creek but turned back and forged into the Sierra Ancha. The strategy of the wily Tontos was to abandon their rancherias, having had full warning of the approach. Then when the army moved in to destroy the village the Indians would surround them on the adjacent hills and fire devastating volleys upon the soldiers. Bourke describes the jungle-like conditions (scrub oak, manzanita and the like), which made the Apache positions all but inaccessible. The soldiers lost what prisoners they had managed to round up "who darted like jackrabbits into the brush and were out of sight in a flash."

Deadly skirmishes between military detachments and the Tontos continued to take place in the Mazatzals and Sierra Ancha. Before he left command of the Arizona Military Department General Ord outlined a plan for an extensive area in eastern Arizona to become a reservation for the White Mountain Apaches. He supposed that after the military established it the Office of Indian Affairs would take over its supervision. He imagined the Apache bands would be isolated on this reserve, soon surrounded by white settlers and ready to follow their example as farmers. He believed this was the only alternative to a continuation of the policy of extermination of the Apaches.

Now in command, General Stoneman was torn by the dilemma of how to deal with this continuing "Apache problem." The Tontos were vexed by an even more severe white problem, but continued to hold the advantage because of the rugged terrain and their style of warfare. The Chiricahua bands in southern Arizona were rampaging so furiously that much of the territory's troop strength had to be concentrated there. Calls for genocide were growing once again but at the same time the power structure in the East called for more peaceful methods of dealing with the Indians. Stoneman was caught between the two opinions. He was firm in his belief that to offer blankets and rations would induce the Apaches to become peaceful. Reservations were the key, he thought, where the Indians could be taught to farm and support themselves.

However, from the civilian point of view there was an economic necessity for keeping the war going and avoiding peace. Apart from mining and cattle, much of Arizona's economy was based on contracts with the government to supply the military posts. Peace would mean less army and fewer contracts. War was lucrative so the many who stood to gain continued the hue and cry for a war of extermination. Peace also meant that Indians farming in the vicinity of military posts would be selling their products to the army, undermining white contractors.

By July, 1870, General Stoneman had charted his plan of action, closely following the ideas left to him by General Ord. It was to develop settlements of citizens large enough to protect themselves against the Apaches, concentrate the troops at fewer posts, consider all Indians not friendly to his plan as hostile, and win the cooperation of the civilians in fighting them. He proposed an extensive area of Eastern Arizona as a permanent reserve for the White Mountain Apaches.

In late July, 1870 the General made a visit to Camp Verde accompanied by the publisher of Prescott's *Arizona Miner*, John Marion. During this visit, Stoneman saw to it that a new road from there to Camp Ord (the future Fort Apache) was begun. The new route, later called the Stoneman Road, was further south than the old Beale route which passed by the San Francisco Peaks. Stoneman's road crossed the Mogollon Plateau at a lower altitude, had fewer volcanic boulders which made travel so difficult, included more watering spots and was 100 miles shorter. Stoneman Lake, which lay along the route, also received its name from the general.

As the colder weather of autumn began to settle over Apacheria, troops were diverted to the south to combat the growing intensity of Chiricahua raids and few forays were launched against the Tontos and their allies. But changes for the Tontos were in the air.

Chapter Thirty-Nine

THE CALL FOR RESERVATIONS

The White Mountain Apaches had made peace with the American Army and agreed to the establishment of a post in the midst of their territory in exchange for food to feed their hungry people. While Col. Green was setting up a post on the north fork of the White River, the Chiricahua chief Cochise visited, stating a desire to make peace with the Americans. To acknowledge his visit, the post was later named Camp Apache. Cochise had experienced a severe defeat in which sixty-one of his warriors were killed and he sought peace until his people could recover. He offered to bring the Chiricahua band onto a reservation if one was created for them.

As colder weather began to settle over the Rim Country the reservation was not forthcoming and Cochise led his people back to the southern mountains where his attacks became more vicious than ever. Troops were diverted from central Arizona to combat the growing intensity of the Chiricahua raids. A temporary reservation for Apaches had been set up at Camp Thomas on the upper and it was the target of Prescott's *Arizona Miner*, sarcastically suggesting that the Indians were "living on the generous bounty of our philanthropic uncle." The paper strongly opposed the idea of reservations. On the other hand, its editor accompanied General Stoneman to visit the White Mountain Apaches and seemed to be ready for compromise. He wrote, "We know it to be the fixed opinion of most Arizonans that the Apache cannot be tamed, but proper measures for doing so have never before been taken, and it may be that this opinion will soon be abandoned. We hope so, at all events, for it is cheaper, better for the country to feed and civilize them than it is to fight them, which latter mode of dealing with them has so far proved an expensive, ineffectual way of subduing them."

Whether for economic or humanitarian reasons this point of view was gaining strong momentum among the powers in Washington. After the 1869 inauguration of President Ulysses S. Grant, a push for peace intensified. There had been growing discontent in the country with the way the Office of Indian Affairs was handling the peace process. The continuing war against the Apaches seemed futile. The weariness of soul which war brings was pressing the American conscience.

At President Grant's behest a board of Indian commissioners was established in June of 1869. In addition to auditing the accounts of the Office of Indian Affairs, they had wide powers to supervise the purchase and transporting of goods given the Indians. The Commission was also charged with visiting the tribes, consulting with the chiefs and Indian agents, and investigating reports of cruelties to Indians. They were to escort parties of Indians to various cities in the North and East in order to champion Indian rights.

The Friends, or Quakers, met with President Grant and suggested he appoint "religious men" as agents and employees to work with the various tribes. It was hoped this would end the spoils system that had ingrained itself among Indian agents across the rest of America. Grant accepted this "Quaker Policy" and appointed various Christian denominations to administrate the reservations.

As yet the Apaches did not have any agents or reservations, except the temporary camp at Fort Thomas, so the peace movement emanating from the eastern United States did not reach Arizona in December of 1870. In that month the Tontos ranged as far south as Tucson, driven by hunger. Seventy-five Tontos attacked a freight train in Canyon del Oro en route from Camp Goodwin to Tucson. Although forty well-armed men guarded the train, the Indians were successful in stealing at least thirty head of oxen. They drove the animals north over the Dripping Springs Mountains across the Salt River and into the Sierra Ancha. There they camped on a high mesa and made jerky of the slaughtered animals. When the site was later found it was named Jerky Butte.

The Sixth Territorial Legislature met in Tucson on January 11, 1871 and Governor Safford's colorful message played well. "The question of paramount importance since the acquisition of the territory has been, and is now, the hostility of the Apache Indians. The history of these Indians is written in blood." He went on to paint a vivid picture of Indian atrocities and praise the fortitude of white settlers. He also stated that the army was totally inadequate to "the prosecution of an energetic, aggressive war and no other kind of war will ever reduce the Apache to submission." He pleaded for memorials that would urge Congress to authorize the raising of another Arizona Volunteer Infantry, by which the Territory's own people could more cheaply "fight for their homes and firesides."

However, the federal government's policy of appeasement was about to be felt in Arizona with an impending change of military leadership. General George Crook was in the wings, about to be assigned to the Military Department of Arizona. He would win the respect of the Apaches and advocate for the establishment of reservations.

Chapter Forty

THE SCENE IS SET FOR CROOK'S CAMPAIGN

The decade of the 1870's was the time of devastation for the Tonto Apache bands. By the end of the decade their land had been wrested from them and their identity as a unique people all but extinguished. The campaign led by General George Crook, from 1871 to 1874, was an intensive crusade by the U. S. Army to starve the tribes into submission and incarcerate them on bounded reserves where their lives could be controlled.

When General Crook took command of the Military Department of Arizona the war against the Indians had been raging for seven years. He was determined to conclude it, and wage a campaign against the tribes that would eliminate them as a threat to white settlement. However, the federal government prevented him from launching an all-out campaign because the strong peace movement gripped Washington. President Grant sided with the "Peace Party" saying, "I do not believe our Creator ever placed different races of men on this earth with the view of having the stronger exert all their energies on exterminating the weaker. If any change takes place in the Indian policy of the government while I hold my present office it will be on the humanitarian side of the question."

The plan was to confine the Indians to reservations where these traditional hunter-gatherers would become farmers. Throughout 1871 the government established reservations around the periphery of Apache Territory and one, Camp Apache, in the midst of it. At Date Creek a reservation was established for the Yavapai and Mojave. At Camp Verde, on the dividing line between Tonto Apache and Yavapai Territories, the Rio Verde Reservation was created. On the lower Verde River the Camp McDowell Reservation was established for Yavapai bands and in 1872 the San Carlos Reservation was established along the Gila River. All Indians were warned to surrender and register on one of the reservations or be considered renegades, liable to be killed on sight.

As General Crook made a grand circle of the military posts, it seemed that the White Mountain Apaches were most amenable to peace. Of course, their reservation in the White Mountains included ancestral lands with room to continue their hunting life. While at Camp Apache the general enlisted several of the chiefs and their warriors to be army scouts. He was aware that "it took an Apache to track down an Apache." Such willingness to betray other Apaches belied the idea of an Apache federation. The bands were committed to looking out for themselves even if it meant going against other Apaches.

Crook saw that getting supplies to Camp Apache required a long trek north from Fort Whipple to follow old trails east and then drop south into the White Mountains.

He determined to create a new military and supply road across the edge of the Mogollon Rim, leading from Fort Whipple to Camp Verde, and then eastward to Camp Apache. In the fall of 1871 the well-posted Tontos saw a military party heading for their country from Camp Apache. None of this section of Arizona had been mapped at that time and Crook was proceeding cautiously with a survey team and a detachment of cavalry. As the party of whites approached the headwaters of the East Verde River, a group of Tonto warriors could see they were at ease admiring the awesome beauty of the view from the Rim. Crook's aide-de-camp, John Bourke, would later write about the vast resources of timber and grass they observed and the details of what happened next.

Fifteen or twenty Tontos hid behind the large girth ponderosa pines and then let fly their powerful arrows. The air was filled with the whizzing of these lethal, feathered sticks, one of which buried itself to the feathers in a pine tree that shielded General Crook. Miraculously for the military personnel who had leaped for cover at the first sound of the attack, none was wounded or killed. The cavalry troops were quickly on the scene and with the explosion of their rifles drove the Indians back into the forest. Two of the Apaches headed for the Rim. Bourke wrote, "There they stood, almost entirely concealed behind a boulder on the very edge of the precipice, their bows drawn to a semi-circle, eyes gleaming with a snaky black fire, their long unkempt hair flowing down over their shoulders, bodies almost completely naked, faces streaked with the juice of the baked mescal and the blood of the deer..."

They fired their arrows one more time and then leaped over the edge of the Rim. The soldiers were certain they had fallen to their chosen death. But upon looking over they saw the natives jumping like mountain sheep from rock to rock down the almost vertical cliff. A shot by General Crook wounded one of them whose arm hung limp and bleeding though he continued to make his escape into the forest below.

Crook's party continued their exploration and upon reaching Fort Whipple the general gave orders for the building of the new road. Throughout 1872 and 1873 crews of soldiers and hired laborers blazed the trail and by 1874 it had been widened enough to accommodate supply wagons. Furthermore, it would serve to quickly disburse cavalry units that could intercept renegade Apaches escaping toward the north.

Chapter Forty One

WHITE ANGER AND APACHE VENGEANCE

As the winter of 1871-1872 clutched the Rim Country in its grip, Tonto Apache chiefs began to bring their families to the several reservations. At first the military commanders assumed this meant the beginning of victory over the Apaches, but in fact the Indians came to take advantage of government provisions and avoid the severe winter weather. Many warriors remained at large to continue their raids on wagon trains and ranches. The advocates of peace in Washington kept General Crook idle, still hoping that the Apaches would capitulate.

Meanwhile, politics dominated the administration of the reservations. A bitter struggle for control of the reservations was going on between the War Department, desiring military control, and the Department of Interior, wanting civilian control. Corrupt Indian agents were taking beef and other supplies from the Indians to sell on a "black market" for their own profit. The Apaches who had gone to the reservations were on the edge of revolt because such practices robbed them of promised food.

Washington sent General Oliver Otis Howard to Arizona with hopes of negotiating peace. Howard was a devout man who knelt publicly for prayer before he held conferences and who was opposed to the practice of genocide. However, by the summer of 1872 even General

Howard had become convinced peace was not possible with the fierce Tonto Apache and Yavapai bands. Even while he held talks with them the Tontos, or perhaps Yavapai, drove off a beef herd from Camp Verde and 2,000 sheep were stolen from within one and a half miles of Fort Whipple. The pursuing cavalry troops caught up with the raiders eighty miles east of the post in Tonto territory and, while most of the Apaches escaped, the cattle and sheep were recovered. In addition, thirty white persons had been killed by Indians during the spring and summer. The Apaches were trading with the Navajos for guns and becoming better armed. A joke going around the territory was that the whites were on the reservation while the Apaches ran the country.

Prescott's *Arizona Miner* on July 6th wrote tongue in cheek poetry:

Some playful Tontos of the House of Delshay

Stole three fatted bullocks and silently fled away.

Apache headman Del-che-ae, whose stronghold was in the Sierra Ancha, had become a hero in the eyes of his brethren, but an infamous renegade in the eyes of the white population.

General Howard moved to consolidate the reservations and had the ones at Date Creek and Camp McDowell abolished, as well as the Hualapai Reservation at Beale Springs. Indians from those reserves were sent to the Rio Verde and newly established San Carlos reservations. As the military forced various tribes to live together within limited boundaries they completely misunderstood the animosity Indians often had toward each other. There was no native federation in Arizona and even though one or another band might surrender, the resistance continued because each band had to be defeated separately.

One of Del-che-ae's wives was Yavapai and this alliance meant his people and his Yavapai in-laws worked together for both raiding and defense. His wife and their son were among some Tontos who went to a reservation to obtain supplies. There the son contracted malaria and upon returning to the mountains he died. Del-che-ae's grief turned to anger and he blamed the boy's mother. He brutally killed her in the presence of her Yavapai relatives. This ended their alliance and the Yavapai band left to camp along the Salt River. There they were discovered by a military detachment and all but a few were killed in what became known as the Battle of the Caves.

General Crook now had a free hand to launch a vigorous campaign. His strategy was for highly mobile troop detachments to move out in several directions supported by pack trains. Each company had thirty to forty Apache scouts commanded by white officers and white scouts. The soldiers would hit the hostiles wherever they could be found, keeping them on the move and bottled up in the mountains where winter would take its toll.

The army took many prisoners and they were incarcerated at the Rio Verde reservation. However, many did not stay put. For example, when the Tontos demanded the commanding officer return their firearms so they could hunt, he refused and all but six left the reservation. Other times they would draw their rations but immediately bolt the reservation to conduct raids on settlers. None of these renegade activities went unchallenged and the cavalry usually caught up with them, killing scores and taking many prisoners throughout 1872 and 1873. So many were killed or captured that in April of 1873 General Crook announced the Tonto Basin phase of his campaign completed.

Del-che-ae, who was still at large, remained a prime target for General Crook. Although his warriors were discovered and killed on several occasions and the women and children captured, the chief continued to escape. Slowly the headmen loyal to Del-che-ae were becoming disillusioned with his leadership and began leading their people to the Rio Verde Reservation for protection. One head man brought 2,300 of his followers in after the hard winter of 1872-73. Then in March of 1873 a major battle occurred against the Tontos on Turret Mountain in the Verde Valley. It signaled the end of Tonto resistance except for one hold out: Del-che-ae.

Chapter Forty Two

THE DEATH OF DELSHAY

In March of 1873 Crook's army, led by army scout C. C. Cooley and his White Mountain Indian company, captured a Tonto woman and forced her to show them where the Tonto warriors were hiding out. The trail led up the treacherous Turret Peak overlooking the Verde River in the Pine Mountain Wilderness. Approaching undetected they attacked the Tonto camp at dawn. Some Tontos jumped off the cliff to their death; fifty others were killed and fifteen taken prisoners.

The Tontos hoped this remote mountain top would be a safe retreat but this defeat broke their spirit. Then throughout April bands of Tonto Apaches and Yavapai began surrendering at the Rio Verde Reservation. As Yavapai chief Chalipun led over two thousand of his people to the reservation he was quoted as saying, "You see, we're nearly dead from want of food and exposure. The copper cartridge has done the business for us. I'm glad of the opportunity to surrender, but I do it not because I love you but because I am afraid of General Crook."

Del-che-ae still held out, defiant with his shrinking band of warriors. On April 23rd an army detachment located his camp in a canyon on the Mogollon Rim and after firing a few shots the chief surrendered with twenty men, the only ones who had stayed with him. Ever the dramatist, he began to cry, promising to follow orders in order to save his people from starvation. He said things like every rock had turned into a soldier, or that the rocks had become soft and left Tonto foot prints that the soldiers could follow.

The renegade band was taken to Camp Apache where they were mistreated and threatened by the White Mountain bands. In the early summer Del-che-ae took his few men and bolted the reservation, only to show up at the Rio Verde reservation asking for food and medicine. The defiant chief set up his camp apart from the main village and immediately began to foment rebellion among the other Tontos. Conditions deteriorated during the summer of 1873 and the Tontos were so weak and sick many of the dead were left unburied to mummify in the dry air. Twenty-two Tontos volunteered to become army scouts, searching for Apaches who had left the San Carlos Reservation and General Crook was proclaiming victory over the Tontos. When the threat of revolt grew strong at Rio Verde the commander was ordered to arrest Del-che-ae to keep him from stirring up rebellion. Several confrontations followed until September when the Tonto chief again escaped with a contingent of malcontented Tontos. Other warrior bands who had never surrendered joined him and the war was back on. For the next nine months army units scouted throughout the Mazatzal Mountains, the Mogollon Rim, and Pine Mountain Wilderness in hot pursuit of the renegades.

During the severe winter of 1873-1874 more Tontos surrendered at San Carlos, begging to be forgiven and taken in. General Crook allowed them to stay on one condition. They had to bring in the heads of their ringleaders, including that of Del-che-ae. During the following months a number of bloody heads were brought to the San Carlos Agency and placed on posts around the parade ground. However, Del-che-ae was still at large. Crook offered to pay $50.00 for his head. Three Tonto scouts came into the Rio Verde Reservation and handed the camp physician, Dr. William Corbusier, a crumpled bloody rag saying, "Del-che-ae." The physician wrote, "On opening the parcel I found a whole scalp with the left ear hanging to it, in the lobe of which was tied a pearl shirt button." Chief Del-che-ae was known to wear this memento in his left ear, taken from some white victim. The scouts claimed to have killed him near Turret Peak on July 29th. However, on August 21st a Tonto warrior named Desalin brought an Apache head to the San Carlos Agency and claimed *it* was Del-che-ae's. The Indians at San Carlos and Camp Verde each tried to persuade General Crook that theirs was the authentic remains of the chief. The diplomatic General wrote, "Being satisfied that both parties were earnest in their beliefs, and the bringing in of an extra head was not amiss, I paid both parties."

The issue was further complicated when a Tonto Apache at San Carlos told Crook the head taken there was his son, not Del-che-ae. Other followers of the chief also testified it was not Del-che-ae's head. The general came to the conclusion that the Camp Verde scalp and ear was authentic and affirmed in his annual report of August 31st, 1874 that "Delshay was killed by his own people near Turret Mountain."

A relatively quiet summer followed as the Apache and Yavapai bands at Rio Verde dug irrigation ditches and harvested hay to sell to the army.

Chapter Forty Three

THE TONTOS' LONG MARCH

Many of America's native tribes had their "trail of tears," a long march forced upon them as they were moved from one territory or another by white armies. The Tontos and Yavapai were no exception.

After General Crook proclaimed the Tonto rebellion quelled, life on the Rio Verde Reservation seemed to proceed smoothly. The Yavapai and Apache families dug irrigation ditches so that a significant tract of land along the Verde River was under cultivation. Soon they were providing food and hay not only for themselves but enough to supply Fort Verde. This did not sit well with a powerful group of politicians and freighters in Tucson whose economic interests were jeopardized. Valuable government contracts for supplying the reservation and the military post in the Verde Valley were being cut and in danger of being eliminated altogether. The special interests in Tucson put pressure on Washington to close down the Rio Verde Reservation and move those Indians to San Carlos. In response, the Bureau of Indian Affairs issued just such an order in February of 1875. The military rounded up the Rio Verde bands and forced them to begin a 150-mile foot march to San Carlos on the Gila River. 1,452 people of all ages set out on the march and they included not only Tonto Apaches and eastern bands of Yavapai, but western Yavapai bands called Mojave-Apache and several Pai groups.

These various tribes had often been at enmity and now under such tension it is no wonder they began to quarrel as they traveled. The march proceeded to the East Verde River and as they approached the mouth of Pine Creek many Tontos began to think they might escape. This was their home territory. High on the palisades that enclosed the river canyon were pre-historic fortresses. The Tontos had used these during the war both to hide out and harass army units passing below along the river trail. During the night several families did slip away and they remained hidden in the labyrinth of mountain canyons for years. Decades later it would be safe to show themselves and reclaim their old campgrounds.

Among the scouts who accompanied the army detachment in the long march were chief packer Sam Hill and Chief of Scouts Al Sieber. Later Sam Hill, then turned prospector, would report to Tonto Forest Ranger Fred Croxen what happened. As the Indians and army personnel camped for the night on the flats by Pine Creek an argument erupted between Yavapai and Tonto bands over which of them had killed a deer. The Indians were required to furnish most of their own food during the march. During the afternoon the Indian boys began throwing rocks at each other. Just before dark Sam Hill went down to the river to wash up and an Indian told him there was going to be a fight that night. Hill reported this to the commanding officer who made light of it. The soldiers and packers had already pitched their camps between the two factions. At dusk the Yavapai and Apaches began shooting at each other, having somehow obtained firearms. Fourteen Indians were killed and were buried along Pine Creek. At least three others who were killed were carried off in the melee by escaping Indians. This site at the junction of Pine Creek and the East Verde River would one day become Mazatzal City, a settlement of Mormons, and still later the homesteads of Payson area cattle ranchers.

A February snow had fallen and the long march continued over ice and through swollen streams. They left the East Verde River at City Creek following a trail the military first put through in 1868. It joined Rye Creek and proceeded down Tonto Creek, then through the Tonto Basin to the Salt River. There the Indians were forced to wade through the flooding Salt River and from there to the unfamiliar territory of San Carlos. They found themselves among other groups who not only had different customs but different dialects. Araviapa, Chiricahua, Tonto, White Mountain, Carrizzo, Cibicue, and Pinal Apaches were thrown in with Mojave, Yavapai, and other Pais. Many of them had at times been enemies and now their captors, who assumed every Indian was like every other Indian, jammed them together.

During the long march some died of illness or were frozen to death. Twenty-five babies were born while mothers were on the march and that many were stillborn or died from exposure. The number reaching San Carlos was about one-hundred fewer than had begun the march.

The next month, March, 1875 General Crook was transferred to the Department of the Platte.

Chapter Forty-Four

LIFE AT SAN CARLOS

No sooner had the Tonto Apache and Yavapai bands been rounded up on the San Carlos Reservation than white homesteaders began staking out the Indian lands for themselves. Those Tontos who escaped the incarceration hid in the canyons of the Mazatzals, Sierra Ancha and Mogollon Rim. Now they observed their homelands being turned into sheep and cattle ranches. Throughout 1875 white settlers took over Greenback Valley, Tonto Basin, Big and Little Green Valley, Round Valley, Pleasant Valley, and many of the fresh water canyons embraced by the Rim. The Tonto hold-outs simply kept out of sight, hoping for a time when they could make peace with the settlers. Their camps often became a refuge for renegade Apaches who left the reservation. Some Tontos who never registered even joined occasional raids on white settlements.

John Clum, the Indian Agent for the White Mountain and San Carlos Reservations, formed a company of Indian Police to keep order and help the cavalry recapture renegades. In the summer of 1875, Clum was ordered by Washington to remove the White Mountain, Cibecue and Ojo Caliente Apaches from their homelands and add them to those already on the San Carlos reservation. The military refused to assist in this move and Clum was left on his own to convince the

Indians to move. He was partially successful but this new influx at San Carlos only worsened the already aggravated situation among rival tribes. Several bands who had pledged peace remained at Camp Apache and many became army scouts. In October the Indian agency at Camp Apache was closed and became a sub-agency of San Carlos. Meanwhile the Chiricahua Reservation in southeastern Arizona was closed so settlers could occupy more tribal land and more Chiricahua Apaches came to San Carlos. The crowded and tense living conditions were almost more than John Clum and his Apache Police could control. In October the military companies at San Carlos left for Camp Bowie where they were chasing Geronimo and his renegades, leaving Clum alone with the Indian Police to keep order at San Carlos.

The ancient traditions of family life and organization quickly began to disintegrate among the Apaches. The government lumped groups together without considering their family traditions and called them "tag-bands" to facilitate the handout of rations. Numbers, or tags, were assigned to individuals as the whites gave up on their Indian names. Tag-band chiefs were appointed by their white overseers from those willing to be amenable to directions without regard for the traditional democratic elections of headmen. Resentment ran high. Not only had these people been forced from ancestral lands where they had ranged free in limitless spaces, now they were crammed together. Most of them had never been associated with one another and they were being forced to change the lifestyles of centuries from hunting and gathering to farming.

By December incidents were occurring in which a chief would rebel and the police would shoot him dead. The police were often blood brothers of the rebels and felt like traitors to their own people. However, the military contingent at Camp Apache was aiding them. A number of the Tontos who were resettled at San Carlos now became army scouts. Among them was a young Tonto named De-a-li-a, often called De-ga-la. He signed up for his first hitch on October 27, 1877 and began a series of reenlistments assigned to various scout companies. He received his honorable discharge from the army in July 1894. During this time his people began to drift off the reservation unopposed to settle in the places where they were born. During his enlistments he experienced many adventures, chasing Geronimo, working for the Buffalo Soldiers (and even stealing their payroll in one daring raid), and fighting with other Tonto scouts at the Battle of Big Dry Wash in 1882. In 1884 he married a San Carlos Apache named Lizzie Anna Nau-to-bog-all. During several of his enlistments he took on the names of his white officers. When they would ask him his name, he would identify himself with that officer's corps, "Me Irving-man" or "Me Evans-man." Consequently he took on the name Henry Irving and later Henry Evans during his service as an army scout. The children of Henry and Lizzie, born during those days, also carried the names Irving or Evans. Henry's progeny continued in the Payson area later to become leaders in the establishment of the Tonto Reservation.

As the 1870s turned to the 1880s conditions at San Carlos were worse than bad. The reservation was a desert wilderness, unlike the grassy and forested mountains Apaches had always occupied. The 4,400 square mile reservation was controlled by the agency located at the confluence of the Gila and San Carlos rivers, which today is under the lake of Coolidge Dam. A few cottonwood trees offered the only shade with temperatures often in the 100 degree range. Dust, gnats, flies, and floods made life miserable. Rations were issued once a week from the agency which meant crossing the rivers, usually flowing up to the horses' bellies. They were not allowed to hunt for game and were entirely dependent on the dole. Life was a fight for survival and tensions were mounting to the point of an explosion.

Chapter Forty Five

VIOLENCE AND REBELLION

In 1881 word was spreading about a mystic of the White Mountain Tribe who was preaching a radical philosophy at Cibecue and Carrizo. His name was Nock-ay-del-klinne. Both White Mountain and Tonto Apaches began slipping away to his meetings to hear his strange message. He prophesied that if they would pray with the demanding Wheel Dance their prayers would cause the resurrection of Apache chiefs who had been killed by the white soldiers. He also predicted that all the whites would die and the Indians would once again claim their lands. One chief who was present at a session with Nock-ay-del-klinne claimed to have seen Mangas Coloradas, Cochise, and Victorio rise in the misty light after the prophet's prayers. That rumor spread rapidly among the malnourished and defrauded bands of Indians.

In an earlier year, 1875, army officer's wife Martha Summerhayes described the wild dances of the White Mountain Apaches in her book *Vanished Arizona*. We can imagine the vivid scene under the influence of the mystic prophet Nock-ay-del-klinne. The army wives looked over the bluff on which Camp Apache was situated to the natural amphitheater below. It blazed with fires and some Apaches sat on logs beating drums. Others danced, naked except for the loincloth; their bodies were painted and feathers stood out on their elbows and knees. Jingling tins and shells were attached to their necks and arms, their heads sprouted elk horns and they twisted and turned wildly in the firelight. As the fire was built higher, the dancers looked alternately like birds or animals or demons. As the shouts and drums grew louder it was terrifying for the observers. Suddenly it all stopped; the arena emptied and two evil looking creatures appeared doing a shadow dance. Once again the tempo and the noise picked up as shouts became whoops and the emotional rhythm increased.

In the summer of 1881 there was growing concern at Camp Apache that this fury would get out of hand. Rumors that the prophet was calling for death to all whites caused the camp commander to march to Cibecue with a company of soldiers intending to arrest Nock-ay-del-kinne. Upon arriving at the prophet's camp, the detachment was surrounded by the medicine man's followers. When one of the soldiers fired on the menacing Indians a bloody skirmish followed. Nock-ay-del-klinne was killed and the Apache warriors disbursed in the face of army firepower, but not until seven soldiers were killed, two others wounded, and many pack mules and horses were missing or killed. The army contingent slowly extracted itself and cautiously returned to the post.

Ripples of this event reverberated throughout the White Mountain and San Carlos reservations. Small groups of soldiers and civilians were attacked and killed by Indians as they carried messages and repaired torn down telegraph lines. The day after the soldiers returned to Camp Apache from Cibecue the post was fired upon from all sides by the Apaches, wounding at least one soldier and setting several buildings on fire. The daylong skirmish ended at nightfall.

After Nock-ay-del-klinne's death, a new rebel leader emerged named Nantiotish. He rallied about eighty others and launched a bloody raid on the ranches in and around Pleasant Valley. Several settlers were killed or wounded and many horses stolen. Agitation continued until July 1882 when the rebellion reached a point of no return. Nantiotish led one hundred warriors and women on a bloody warpath. Two renegade parties left the reservation, one attacking the gold rush town of McMillenville. The territorial government had taken that area out of the reservation because of coveted mineral rights. The other party led by Nantiotish headed again for Pleasant Valley, killing more settlers and stealing horses. The two parties joined to leave a trail of burning ranches and dead settlers in the canyons under the Mogollon Rim and up the East Verde River. Climbing the Rim the Apaches planned an ambush at East Clear Creek, a place the army called the Big Dry Wash. Cavalry units from the surrounding military posts converged to fight the last major Apache battle to be waged on Arizona soil, the Battle of Big Dry Wash. At least eighty Indians were killed, including Nantiotish. Six were captured while others escaped and anonymously filtered back to the reservation. One white soldier was killed and buried at the site. Also one Tonto scout was killed, Haski-ta-go-loth, called "Pete" by the military. He was the brother of Tonto scout Sgt. Smiley who also fought at Big Dry Wash. Along with these men, Henry Evans and several other Tonto Apaches were on both sides of the fight. Some had joined the renegades, others as scouts fought with the army.

Chapter Forty Six

THE RETURN HOME

As the 19th century entered its last decade, military control over the San Carlos Reservation became lax. Tonto and Yavapai families found themselves free to return to the places they called home and this usually meant returning to the places where their fathers were born. Those men who served as Army scouts were given passes and little was done to stop others who wished to leave. A new generation had been born on the reservation and some Tontos who married into White Mountain, Cibecue, or San Carlos families preferred to remain behind. Others drifted back to Payson, Rye, Gisela, Fossil Creek, and the Verde Valley. There they found that their traditional lands occupied by white ranchers so they made their camps where they could, usually poaching on lands that were in the process of becoming national forests.

To sustain their lives in the old ways of living off the land was impossible. The settlers were decimating much of the big game, but hunting deer and elk produced an occasional kill. The Tontos harvested agave hearts to roast in pits, pinion nuts and acorns in season, and cut grasses for baskets. The children became adept at catching pack rats, which became a staple in the Tonto camps. However, for the major part of their livelihood the Tontos now became dependent upon the white homesteaders and hired out as laundresses, woodchoppers, or cowboys.

They also found employment in some of the mines around Payson and after the turn of the century many found work building the new roads that county governments were constructing to link white communities.

In the Payson area a Tonto camp was located near the mouth of Rye Creek where it empties into Tonto Creek, just below the narrows where later the Bush Highway would cross with a steel span bridge. For generations the Tontos had periodically occupied this campsite and it was there that Melton Campbell, later to become headman for the Payson area Tontos, was born in 1941. His sister, Vinnie Ward, was also born there as were a number of cousins. The camp was on a flat overlooking the creek where a spring brought fresh water from the hillside. The fertile land flanking the creek produced good crops of corn, squash and watermelons. An orchard of peach trees was planted and mesquite beans were plentiful. Metates in the rocks, used for grinding the beans, were also plentiful, many dating to pre-Apache times. A water ditch, drawn from upstream, followed the north side of the river to irrigate the crops. Modern petroglyphs reflect recent usage by the Tontos. One inscription reads "Wally Davis 1961." However, after World War II this camp was abandoned except for its cemetery, as those who were left moved to Payson's Indian Hill.

In the 1920s and 1930s when Julian Journigan was driving the mail between Payson and Globe, the Tontos ordered goods from pictures in the Sears catalogue. These the mail carrier graciously delivered. Social life flourished on Indian Hill as there were two other Tonto camps nearby. The families at these camps worked cooperatively to maintain their hay fields and harvest their crops, as well as to conduct their dances and social events. One of those was upstream on Tonto Creek at Gisela.

Leadership in the Gisela camp centered around a medicine man and patriarch named Silver Allen. He had weathered the Long March in 1875 from Rio Verde to San Carlos and like many other Tontos had been an army scout; thus the federal government had given him a parcel of land in recognition of his service. For many years Silver Allen performed as the doctor and spiritual leader for the camps in the Payson area. Because he owned the property he was allowed to put up a fence line and he kept a small herd of horses. He used to ride his black gelding named Nick up through Payson to visit and shop. However, he did not have a grazing permit from the Forest Service and when Silver Allen grew old and could no longer ride they confiscated the animals. One month when he missed picking up his paycheck at the Payson post office, the postmaster went to Gisela looking for him. He was found dying of malnutrition and pneumonia. They took him in a jeep to the San Carlos Indian Hospital where he died. He was buried at San Carlos. After nearly all the Tontos left the Gisela camp the government took over their land near the Gisela cemetery.

Another scout, Capt. Smiley, who fought in the Battle of Big Dry Wash was from the Gisela camp, as were a number of other Tonto scouts. In the early 1900s another large migration of Tontos took place from San Carlos to the Payson area because massive flooding on the Gila River and its tributaries had wiped out so many of the farms. Adding insult to injury, in 1918 many Tonto lives were taken by the world-wide flu epidemic. From then on Tonto camps around Payson were abandoned except for occasional crop gathering in season. The Tonto families needed to live where employment was available. The building of Roosevelt Dam and new roads in the Tonto Basin took many families to the place called "Where The Waters Run Together," the convergence of Tonto Creek with the Salt River. Later the development of a sawmill in Payson provided some jobs for many years. Indian Hill became a permanent camp for Tonto Apaches.

Chapter Forty Seven

EAST VERDE AND INDIAN HILL

One of the Tonto camps that flourished near Payson in the first half of the 20th century was on the East Verde River just below the crossing of State Route 87. Two more ephemeral camps were located at Flowing Springs and at the mouth of Webber Creek, but white ranches soon occupied those places. The leader of this East Verde band of Tonto Apaches was Delia Cabbelechia. English-speaking people could not pronounce her name so she was called Delia Chapman. More often it was simple Dee-lee.

There were about fifty Tontos in this community. Around 1904 the Office of Indian Affairs (later to become the Bureau of Indian Affairs) arranged with the newly organized Forest Service to set aside 160 acres of this camp for the Tonto Apaches. This was done ostensibly to compensate those families whose men had served as army scouts during the campaigns of the 1870s and 1880s. The unspoken hope of the settlers was that this would keep the Indians from settling in Payson. The deal was negotiated by the Payson Justice of the Peace, George Randall (father of Julia Randall who became Payson's long tenured school teacher). In Apache tradition the women not only were strong leaders but were the owners of family property. Delia's name was put on the deed.

From the East Verde camp it was relatively easy for the members to commute to Payson for employment. Delia worked as a laundress for Mrs. William Hilligas. However, the depression in the 1930s forced the Tontos to leave the East Verde camp because work became so scarce. During those difficult economic times some returned to San Carlos or the Middle Verde camp in the Verde Valley, while others joined the group living on Indian Hill. Delia sold her land for $500 to Roy Blevins and in 1941 he filed the homestead claim that would become the East Verde Estates.

It was in 1915 that some of the East Verde families as well as others from San Carlos moved to Payson and established the camp on Indian Hill, north of Main Street. It was there the Evans, Burdette, Irving and Bread families found their way into the good graces of early Payson residents. Water was obtained from wells along Main Street whose owners invited the Tontos to help themselves.

Among the Tonto Apaches living on Indian Hill were the families of Henry Burdett and Henry Irving. These men were the maternal and paternal forbears of Melton Campbell who would later become "Chief" Campbell and their progeny would become leaders in the Tonto Tribe. Burdett was born and raised in the Payson area. His Indian name was "Chitten," meaning *ashes* or *charcoal*. As we have seen Irving was a man with several names because during different hitches in the army he took on the name of his white officer. One was Campbell, another Irving, and another was Evans. His children carried the name he was using when they were born. His Apache name was De-ay-li-a, which Sergeant Smiley said means "anything that does not grow tall," but Henry used to say he did not know what it meant.

The old road to Pine that crossed Indian Hill cut the camp in two. The east side, above today's high school, was where they buried their dead. The west side was where they built their humble houses. Because the Apaches traditionally considered the land as belonging to Usen (God) and their living on the land a sacred right as part of the Creation, it was not in their tradition to "own property." However, Henry Irving understood the American civilization enough from his army days to know he needed ownership of his family's plot on Indian Hill. He had a small pension from the army and was able to purchase a couple of lots for $20.00, receiving a trustee's deed on July 18, 1930. The other families continued living on the hill without such formalities except they thought Henry's presence there was their security because "he had a paper."

Henry did not stay at Indian Hill as consistently as the Burdetts, but came and went, moving to various camps at Fossil Creek, San Carlos, and Camp Verde. One of his daughters, Mrs. Mary Beecher, lived at Camp Verde and in 1938 Henry formally listed that as his address.

However, Henry did not understand that he had to record his deed at the county courthouse in Globe and that was never done. He paid his taxes each year until 1938 when he moved to his daughter's home at Camp Verde. (Henry died at his daughter's home on November 7, 1941.) The other families, still living on Indian Hill, did not know they had to pay taxes on those lots. From 1938 to 1944 Henry Irving's lots were placed on the county's delinquent tax rolls and on February 5, 1945 Mr. Newell Fuller purchased Henry's property for $3.43, the amount of the lien.

The Tonto families did not know about this and continued to live there until 1954. The town of Payson was expanding and the view from Indian Hill made the property valuable for housing. It was sold to a developer.

The family of Alan Curtis saw the handwriting on the wall and moved to another traditional camp location, south of town. Others followed when white families built on Indian Hill and the last Tontos to leave were members of the Campbell family. In 1957 while they were away visiting Melton Campbell's dad, George Campbell, the developer brought in a bulldozer and leveled their house before they could rescue any of their furniture or personal belongings. The Indian graves were also destroyed.

Chapter Forty Eight

THE CAMP

It was simply called "The Camp," located in the Tonto National Forest south of Payson. When the Tonto Apaches were forced to move there from Indian Hill a Forest Ranger tried to stop it. Allen Curtis stood his ground with a shotgun and said, "Over my dead body." The ranger retreated and the Tonto people created their village west of the highway.

Martha Johnson, the mother of Melton Campbell, made a decisive statement. "And now again, the white man tells us that we must move. They always want something, and they never leave nothing for the Indians, who always called this place their home. In the old days, when I was small, we could move and live wherever we wanted to. There was no people to order us around. Again, they're trying to force us off this land. But we're determined now that we're going to stay and fight. They want us to move back to San Carlos, but I'm never going to move away. I'm going to live here!"

And they did. They had no power, phone or water. For any emergency someone had to run to town and get the fire department or sheriff or doctor. In the first few years five houses were lost to fire. Garbage had to be hauled a mile away to the dump or buried or burned. The butane lanterns they used were considered a great improvement over the kerosene lamps of Indian Hill. They heated and cooked with primitive wood stoves and in summer cooked outside on portable gas stoves. Water was carried in milk cans or empty fuel cans with borrowed pickups. Water was obtained at the sawmill in the hope of finding somebody with a pickup willing to run it out.

The Payson sawmill was the Tontos' primary source of income. They appreciated the generous attitude of their employers where if a man missed a day of work he could go right back to the job the next day. At San Carlos, the mill operators made an employee miss a whole week of work if he failed to show up one day. In Payson the Owens brothers and later Kaibab Industries, the sawmill owners, allowed the Tontos to freely take all the discarded and scrap wood they wanted. Again, a pickup truck would have to be commandeered.

Vinnie Ward, Melton Campbell's sister, worked in town doing laundry, housecleaning and cooking, as did some of the other women. There was a general feeling of not wanting to invest any of their small incomes into fixing up roads or houses at the Camp because they did not own the land. The Tontos gradually felt an identity apart from the Apaches living at San Carlos. Chief Campbell said in 1970, "We are not desert people and we are not farmers. Even today I cannot go down to San Carlos and live." He would go to visit relatives for a day or two but could not stand the air and "there are too many Indians." He felt like a stranger, and the continued drinking at San Carlos turned him off. However, family members from San Carlos would move up to Payson to join their clan.

The Forest Service finally gave up trying to evict them and overlooked the presence of the camp as long as the people did not cut wood or allow animals to run lose on forest property. Livestock had to be penned up. There was a certain amount of pressure on the government to allow them to remain because their labor was needed for the mill, the mines and the local householders. At the camp there were about 80 people, few of whom had never been enrolled on a reservation. A Tonto Apache from San Carlos named Lily Swift moved to The Camp because she was an aunt of Allen Curtis' wife. George Campbell built her a house for which she paid him only half of the agreed price. It was four rooms, the largest house in the Camp. Lily Swift was very zealous for her Christian faith and held Bible studies in her home and directed the building of a brush arbor shelter for services.

One year the Rev. Mr. and Mrs. J. O. Martin arrived from Oklahoma saying they had been called of God to come and serve the Apaches. Pastor Martin was an evangelical preacher who won the hearts of the Tontos and soon he and his wife became much loved. Under his leadership the community built a wooden church that also became a community center. They even acquired a generator to light the building.

After the Martins arrived, Lily Swift returned to San Carlos. Pastor Martin had a profound influence on

The Camp. Among other things, his evangelistic message brought sobriety to the people. Previously there had been much drunkenness. While the Indians were not allowed to buy liquor in town, they often sent non-Indian friends to buy it for them. While on Indian Hill the drunkenness became a severe problem and continued at The Camp. Vinnie Ward said, "Some of them used to drink all day and all night, and never got sobered up until about Tuesday."

The fellowship of the church and Martin's message of salvation through faith in Christ enabled them to stop the drinking. Vinnie Ward said this was not because there were rules against it, but because "it's just best not to drink... I guess they make a vow to God that they wouldn't drink no more." She said her husband would not go to visit at San Carlos after he stopped drinking because they were still drinking all the time down there.

This change freed up the whole community both economically and in their ability to pursue independence. After J. O. Martin left, he passed the mantle of spiritual leadership to one of his protégés, Melton Campbell. When Campbell was a young boy he had come under the influence of Payson teacher Julia Randall. She encouraged the Indian boys to attend school and Melton Campbell was one of the first to do so. While in school, the white kids nicknamed him "Chief" and the sobriquet stayed with him the rest of his life. As an adult he grew into the title.

Several of the local families in Payson took a special interest in the Tontos and sought to better their lives. One of the most active was Mrs. Lewis Pyle. Nanette Smith Pyle was independently wealthy, having come from the East with an inheritance. She married rancher Lewis Pyle. She initiated a day care facility called the Small Fry Day Care and had a building constructed so that the Indian children could be brought in for preschool. Later she was able to get the government to bring a Head Start program to Payson and gave the building to the School District for the town's first kindergarten.

She also enlisted the support of the Save The Children Fund. Each child of a needy family received $100 a year, paid quarterly, for school clothes and books. Fifteen children received this help. Twenty dollars of each $100 was set aside by the community for improvements such as gravel for the roads. During the hard snowfalls in the winters of 1967 and 1968 Nan Pyle rounded up food, blankets and Coleman heaters for the Camp and hired a truck to break through drifts of snow to deliver them.

Awareness of the Tonto Apaches' plight was gaining much attention among the non-Indian citizens and great events were about to happen.

Chapter Forty Nine

THE DREAM COMES TRUE

The continuing friendship of Nan Pyle with the Tonto Apaches led to an effort to help them become economically independent. She built an Art Center on Main Street in Payson used also as a place where arts and crafts could be manufactured and offered for sale. She helped the Indians make the things and then purchased them for sale in the Art Center store. Polly Davis was an outstanding bead maker and, together with others, they produced several print designs that were sold to the Burlington Mills. The milling company produced a line of bed sheets, towels and blankets that provided royalties for the community. Chief Campbell was self-taught in designing and sewing attractive shirts, leisure suits and dresses. He said, "We want to make our own prints and use the best quality textiles. We intend to use the old art forms for new fashions, and are studying the traditional design motifs on baskets, leather and beadwork."

Later when times changed, the tribe's business aptitude would take them in different directions as the laws permitted casinos on reservations.

The population in The Camp was growing and the tribe grew restless with their conditions. They wanted to press the government for title to their few acres. Doris Sturgis and Nan Pyle were prime movers on behalf of the

Payson area Tonto people. They initiated meetings of interested citizens along with members of the tribe and met monthly at the Ox Bow Inn or in the church at The Camp. They tried to get newspaper coverage from Phoenix on the plight of the Indians, but got no response.

The coalition relied heavily on Melton Campbell who had good English and was a natural leader. He had been accepted as pastor of the Full Gospel Church, a successor to Joe Martin. The monthly meetings of the citizens' committee became an ad-hoc governing board for the community at the Camp. They "elected" Melton Campbell the chairman of the tribe and the rest of the community accepted his leadership by common consent. After all he had always been called "Chief" and his father, George Campbell, had been the unofficial leader of the community.

The families agreed that one of the rules for the Camp would be that no new Indians could move in unless they were employed. Doris Sturgis interviewed some of the Indians and wrote articles for the newspaper and letters to congressmen and senators with the story of how much the army scouts had done for the government and their current plight in not having land. Everyone agreed that continued charity was not the answer for the future of the Tontos. They needed to have their own land and the opportunity to become self-sufficient. So the idea of a land exchange came into being.

As it was, the Payson Tontos were not recognized as a tribe by the government and thus were not eligible for medical care and other assistance from the BIA. It was necessary to establish proof of their unique tribal identity. A grant was made by the Doris Duke foundation for a graduate student from the University of Arizona to conduct extensive oral histories among the community members, as well as the elders among white settlers who had dealt with the Tontos for decades. These interviews were conducted by Nicholas P. Houser and remain a primary source of information about the Tonto Tribe.

The leaders retained Joe Sparks, an attorney from Phoenix, to assemble a document on the history of the tribe to prove that these people were separate and distinct from other Apache groups already recognized by the government. These studies would have great persuasive power. In an effort to press the government for help the committee sent a delegation to Washington D.C. to plead their case. Included in the group was Chief Melton Campbell, spokesperson for the tribe. In Washington they made contact with Senators Paul Fannin and Carl Hayden, as well as Representative Sam Steiger. The TV stations in Washington picked up the story of what they called "the lost tribe" and Chief Campbell appeared on talk shows. He also met with President Nixon and Vice President Spiro Agnew, explaining that his people were asking for an 85 acre reservation. The Chief, growing politically astute, subtly suggested such an action would preclude his people from suing the government for millions of dollars in damages as other tribes had successfully done.

Agnew was able to secure a $10,000 grant from the government that was to be held for building infrastructure once the tribe owned their own land. They also needed money appropriated by the government to buy land that could be exchanged for their use. Lewis and Nan Pyle had planned to give their 60 acre Sunflower Ranch to the Girl Scouts but were persuaded to support the needs of the Indians. The Forest Service suggested the Pyle ranch, valued at $1,000 an acre, would only produce 24 ½ acres in exchange and they offered a location east of town at Turkey Springs. The Indians refused this offer because it was not enough land and it was too far away from town. How could they get to work, or even haul water from the spring?

The committee pressed for land across the highway from The Camp though the homeowners to the north, over the hill, raised a strong objection because they feared "their land value would go down and they didn't want Indians crossing their properties." However, after all the publicity and pressure was brought to bear, Congress acted with unusual dispatch and voted in favor of a new reservation on October 6, 1972, officially recognizing the Tonto Apache Tribe. A member of the Forest Service was directed to wait on Chief Campbell with this message, "You may choose any land you wish in Gila County that is under the U. S. Forest Service jurisdiction and it will be yours."

Incidentally, the Pyles later donated their 60 acre ranch for the building of the Lewis Pyle Memorial Hospital and in years to come that meant the Apaches had medical care close by. The tract of hilly land directly across from the Camp was chosen for the reservation. It would be an easy walk to town for work and to shop.

Both Indians and whites marked the irony of that hour. It took one hundred and one years from the time the first reservations were established in Arizona to acknowledge the existence of a people after whom the Tonto National Forest had been named back in 1905. They who had roamed this entire region at will for hundreds of years; now a little more than an acre for each member of their tribe had been returned to the Tonto Apaches.

THE END

EPILOGUE

In 1999 the Tonto Apache Tribe received an additional 272 acres in a deal with the U.S. Forest Service. The additional acreage will allow for additional housing for members of the tribe who wish to live on the reservation. The current population is approximately 140.

Today, the Mazatzal Hotel and Casino is the main economic activity on the reservation. The casino first opened in 1993 in a trailer. The first building was opened in 1995 and the current hotel and casino opened in August 2007. The hotel/casino is one of the largest employers in Payson and the Tribe regularly donates profits from the operation to local groups in need.

Vivian Burdette, daughter of Code Talker Paul Burdette (see below), received the Arizona Culture Keeper award from the Arizona Historical Foundation in April 2003. She was among the first ten recipients of the eventual 100 recipients of the award which was presented up until the Arizona State Centennial in 2012. Vivian was the Chairwoman of the Tonto Apache Tribe at the time and received the award for directing casino gaming revenue to improve economic conditions on the reservation and restoring pride in the Tribe's culture.

Tonto Apache Tribe Awarded Code Talker Coin

The U.S. Mint produces a variety of national medals to commemorate significant historical events or sites and to honor those whose superior deeds and achievements have enriched U.S. history or the world. Under the Code Talkers Recognition Act of 2008, twenty-five Native American tribes were awarded Congressional Gold Medals in recognition of the dedication and valor of the Native American Code Talkers to the U.S. Armed Services during World Wars I and II. Code Talkers were those Native Americans who used their tribal languages as a means of secret communication during wartime.

The design of each coin was unique to the specific tribe to whom it was awarded. Gold medals were presented to the tribe; silver duplicate medals were presented to the specific Code Talkers, their next of kin, or other personal representatives; and bronze duplicates of the medals were made available for sale to the public. Paul Burdette was a member of the Tonto Apache Tribe who served as a Code Talker during World War II. It was his service that designated the Tonto Tribe to be the recipient of a Congressional Gold Medal.

Paul was born in 1921 in Rye, Arizona. He married Rose Clem, a Tonto Apache from Camp Verde, Arizona. The family reported that Paul went to the San Carlos Apache Reservation to enroll so he would be able to join the U.S. Army. His service began on November 10, 1942.

Each Code Talker had a "code name". Paul's was "Rebel". The Code Talkers worked in teams of two and Paul's partner was Nelson Danford, a member of the White Mountain Apache Tribe. Nelson's code name was "Tarter". Many of the Code Talkers abided by the code of silence after the war and never spoke of their role in the war effort.

Paul was honorably discharged from the U.S. Army on November 25, 1945. When the Tonto Apache Tribe was granted federal recognition in 1972, Paul disenrolled with the San Carlos Apache Tribe and enrolled as a member of the Tonto Apache Tribe. Paul passed away on May 28, 1986 at the age of 65.

In May 2012 Paul's daughter, Vivian Burdette, received a telephone call from Eugene Talas, Director of the Hopi Guidance Center and a retired Chief Master Sergeant from the U.S. Air Force. He informed Vivian of her father's participation in World War II as a Code Talker. In June 2013, Vivian was contacted by Betty Birdsong, Program Specialist for the Office of Design from the U.S. Department of the Treasury and informed of plans to present a Code Talker coin to the Tonto Apache Tribe based upon her father's military service as a Code Talker during World War II.

The main side of the coin for the Tonto Apache Tribe depicts a close-up and background view of a Code Talker communicating a message and running a message.

The reverse side features a variation of the Tonto Apache Seal, depicting four feathers, a streak of stylized lightning as depicted in Apache art, and four streamers.

Bibliography

Agenbroad, Larry D. *Before the Anasazi: Early Man on the Colorado Plateau*. Flagstaff, Ariz.: Museum of Northern Arizona, 1990. Print.

Allyn, Joseph Pratt, and John Nicolson. *The Arizona of Joseph Pratt Allyn: Letters from a Pioneer Judge--observations and Travels, 1863-1866*. Tucson: U of Arizona, 1974. Print.

Altshuler, Constance Wynn. *Cavalry Yellow & Infantry Blue: Army Officers in Arizona between 1851 and 1886*. Tucson, Ariz.: Arizona Historical Society, 1991. Print.

Altshuler, Constance Wynn. *Chains of Command: Arizona and the Army, 1856-1875*. Tucson, Ariz. (949 E. 2nd St., Tucson 85719): Arizona Historical Society, 1981. Print.

Altshuler, Constance Wynn. *Starting with Defiance: Nineteenth Century Arizona Military Posts*. Tucson, Ariz.: Arizona Historical Society, 1983. Print.

Ball, Eve, and Nora Henn. *Indeh, an Apache Odyssey*. Provo, Utah: Brigham Young UP, 1980. Print.

Bandelier, Adolph Francis Alphonse, and Charles H. Lange. *The Southwestern Journals of Adolph F. Bandelier, 1880-1882*. Albuquerque: U of New Mexico, 1970. Print.

Barnes, Will C., and Byrd H. Granger. *Arizona Place Names*. Tucson: U of Arizona, 1960. Print.

Basso, Keith H. *Wisdom Sits in Places: Landscape and Language among the Western Apache*. Albuquerque: U of New Mexico, 1996. Print.

Bender, Averam Burton, and Homer Aschmann. *A Study of Western Apache Indians, 1846-1886.* Vol. V. New York: Garland Pub., 1974. Print.

Brodhead, Michael. *Elliott Cous and the Apaches.* The Journal of Arizona History. Summer (1973). Print.

Brown, Stanley C. *The Bakers of Baker's Butte.* The Journal of Arizona History. Autumn. (1996): 253.

Brown, Stanley C. *The One Year War of Company E, Arizona Volunteer Infantry.* Tucson, Ariz.: Tucson Corral of the Westerners, 1997. Print.

Browne, J. Ross. *A Tour through Arizona, 1864: Or Adventures in the Apache Country.* Tucson: Arizona Silhouettes, 1951. Print.

Bourke, John Gregory. *On the Border with Crook.* Lincoln: U of Nebraska, 1971. Print.

Brugge, David M. "A Linguistic Approach to Demographic Problems: The Tonto-Yavapai Boundary." *Ethnohistory*: 355. Print.

Buchanan, Kimberly Moore. *Apache Women Warriors.* El Paso, Tex.: Texas Western, U of Texas at El Paso, 1986. Print.

Byrket, James W. *The Palatkawapi Trail.* Plateau Magazine Vol. 59 #4 1988. Print.

Carr, C.C.C. *A Cavalry Man in Indian Country.* Ashland, Or.: Lewis Osborne Press, 1974. Print.

Carson, Kit, and Blanche C. Grant. *Kit Carson's Own Story of His Life as Dictated to Col. and Mrs. D.C. Peters about 1856-57.* Taos, N.M., 1955: Kit Carson Memorial Foundation. Print.

Carter, Harvey L., and Kit Carson. *Dear Old Kit; the Historical Christopher Carson,* Norman: U of Oklahoma, 1968. Print.

Chapot, Donald. *Babes in Arms.* The Journal of Arizona History. Autumn (1972). Print.
Comfort, Will Levington. *Apache.* Lincoln: U of Nebraska, 1986. Print.

The Cibicue Apache. Prospect heights, IL: Waveland Press Inc., 1986. Print.

Clifton, Henry. *Report of Woolsey's Second Expedition.* Arizona Miner. May 11, 1864. Print.

Conner, Daniel Ellis. *Joseph Reddeford Walker and the Arizona Adventure.* Norman: U of Oklahoma, 1956. Print.

Cook, F.A. *War and Peace: Two Arizona Diaries, Part 1, War.* New Mexico Historical Review. April (1949). Print.

Corbusier, William T. *The Apache-Yumas and Apache-Mojaves.* The American Antiquarian, 1886: 8(5) 276-284; 8(6) 325-339. Print

Corbusier, William T. *Verde to San Carlos; Recollections of a Famous Army Surgeon and His Observant Family on the Western Frontier, 1869-1886.* Tucson, Ariz.: D.S. King, 1969. Print.

Cordero, Lt. Col. *Cordero's Description of the Apache.* New Mexico Historical Review. Vol. 34, #4 (1957). Print.

Cremony, John C. *Life among the Apaches*. Lincoln: U of Nebraska, 1983. Print.

Crook, George, and Martin Ferdinand Schmitt. *General George Crook His Autobiography*. Pbk. ed. Norman: U of Oklahoma, 1986. Print.

Dosh, Deborah S., Duane Klinner, and Inc Research. *An Overview of the Payson Basin Geographic Study Area: Payson and Pleasant Valley Ranger Distrits, Tonto National Forest, Gila County, Arizona*. Flagstaff, Ariz.: Northland Research, 1993. Print.

Effland, Richard Wayne, Barbara S. Macnider, and Ltd Services. *An Overview of the Cultural Heritage of the Tonto National Forest*. Tempe, Ariz.: Archaeological Consulting Services, 1991. Print.

Ellis, Goerge M. *Kit Carson and Ewing Young: The California Expedition of 1929-1930*. San Diego, Ca.: Brand Book #3, San Diego Corral of the Westerners, 1973. Print.

Elson, Mark, and Douglas B. Craig. *The Rye Creek Project: Archaeology in the Upper Tonto Basin*. Tucson, Ariz.: [Center for Desert Archaeology], 1992. Print.

Emory, W.H. *Notes of a Military Reconnaissance: A Study of Arizona's Gila River, 1846*. Tucson, Ariz.: Tucson Corral of the Westerners, Fall 1996. Print.

Emory, William H. *Lieutenant Emory Reports: A Reprint of Lieutenant W.H. Emory's Notes of a Military Reconnoissance [reconnaissance]*. Albuquerque: U of New Mexico, 1951. Print.

Farish, Thomas Edwin. *History of Arizona*. Phoenix, Ariz.: [publisher Not Identified], 1915. Print.

Favour, Alpheus H. *Old Bill Williams*. [New ed. Norman: U of Oklahoma, 1962. Print.

Ferg, Alan. *Western Apache Material Culture: The Goodwin and Guenther Collections*. Tucson, Ariz.: Published for Arizona State Museum, U of Arizona by U of Arizona, 1987. Print.

Genealogy Records of the First Arizona Volunteer Infantry Regiment. Pueblo, Co.: Roan Horse Press, nd. Print [found in AZ Historical Soc. Library-Tucson]

Goddard, Pliny Earle. *Indians of the Southwest*. 4th ed. New York: American Museum of Natural History, 1931. Print.

Goddard, Pliny Earle. ": Myths and Tales from the San Carlos Apache . *Anthropological Papers of the American Museum of Natural History*, XXIV, Part I: Print.

Goodwin, Grenville, and Morris Edward Opler. *Grenville Goodwin among the Western Apache; Letters from the Field*. Tucson: U of Arizona, 1973. Print.

Goodwin, Grenville. *The Social Organization of the Western Apache*. Chicago: U of Chicago Press, 1942. Print.

Goodwin, Grenville. *Western Apache Raiding and Warfare,*. Tucson: U of Arizona, 1971. Print.

Genung, Dan B. *Death in His Saddlebags: Charles Baldwin Genung, Arizona Pioneer*. Manhattan, Kan.: Sunflower UP, 1992. Print.

Gifford, Edward Winslow. *The Southeastern Yavapai*, Berkeley, Calif.: U of California [Press], 1932. Print.

Goff, John S. *King S. Woolsey*. Cave Creek, Ariz.: Black Mountain, 1981. Print.

The Guns in Arizona's Past. Arizona Highways Magazine, April 1969. Print.

Hammond, Susan Hazen. "El Coronel: Jose Franciso Chaves." *Arizona Highways* Jan. 1990: 14f. Print.

Haskell, J. Loring. *Southern Athapaskan Migration A.D. 200-1750*, Tsaile, AZ: Community College Press, 1987. Print. [Navajo]

Hinton, Thomas B. *The Yavapai-Apache Community of the Verde Valley, Arizona*. Unpublished Manuscript. Arizona State Museum Archives [Folder A-1167]. Tucson, AZ, 1953.

Hodge, Frederick Webb. *Handbook of American Indians North of Mexico*. Washington: G.P.O., 1907. Print.

Hohmann, John W. 88, w/Chas. L. Redman, *Continuing Studies In Payson Prehistory*, Anthropological Field Studies, #21, Office of Cultural Resource Management, Department of Anthropology, Arizona State University, Tempe, 1988.

Horr, David A. (ed.). *A Study Of The Apache Indians, Part V: Tonto and Western Apaches*, in Apache Indians IV. NY: Garland Publishing Inc. 327-645. 1974. Print.

Horr, David A. (ed.) *A Study Of Yavapai History*, in Yavapai Indians, NY. Garland Publishing Inc. pp 23-354. Print.

Houser, Nicolas P. 71, oral interviews, *The Doris Duke Indian History Project*, taken by Houser in the Payson, Arizona, area 1971-1972. Tapes are from the Arizona State Museum, Tucson, Arizona. Transcripts are located in the Rim Country Museum Library, Payson, Arizona.

Hunt, Aurora. *Major General James Henry Carleton, 1814-1873, Western Frontier Dragoon*. Glendale, California: A.H. Clark, 1958. Print.

Items Concerning the Tonto Apaches since 1875. Unpublished Manuscript. Arizona State Museum Archives [Folder A-1167]. Tucson, AZ, 1955.

John Udell, The Rest Of The Story, Tales of the Beale Road Publishing Co, Flagstaff, AZ, 1987. Print.

KV Transmission Line. 1981. MS 80-85. Tonto National Forest Supervisor's Office, Phoenix.

Kaywaykla, James, and Eve Ball. *In the Days of Victorio; Recollections of a Warm Springs Apache*. Tucson: U of Arizona, 1970. Print.

Kelly, George Henderson. *Legislative History Arizona 1864-1912*. Phoenix: [Manufacturing Stationers], 1926. Print.

Kessel, William Burkhardt. *White Mountain Apache Religious Cult Movements: A Study in Ethnohistory*. 1976. Print.

Khera, S. *Yavapai: Handbook of North American Indians*. Washington DC: Smithsonian Institution, 1983. Print.

Littell, Norman M. **Indian Claims Commission Report: Proposed Findings On Behalf of the Navajo Tribe of Indians In The San Carlos/Northern Tonto Overlap**, Dockets 22-D, 22-J, Library of the Museum of New Mexico, Division of Anthropology. [Copy in archive of White Mountain Apache Tribe, White River, Arizona.]

Lockwood, Frank C. *The Apache Indians*. Lincoln: U of Nebraska, 1987. Print.

McCarty, Kieran. *Desert Documentary: The Spanish Years, 1767-1821*. Tucson: Arizona Historical Society, 1976. Print.

Macnider, Barbara S., Ltd Services, and J. Scott Wood. *Tonto National Forest Cultural Resources Assessment and Management Plan*. Phoenix: Archaeological Consulting Services, 1989. Print.

Mails, Thomas E. *The People Called Apache*. Englewood Cliffs, N.J.: Prentice-Hall, 1974. Print.

The Medicine Men of the Apache, Ninth Annual Report of the Bureau Of Ethnology, 1887-88, Reprint by Rio Grande Press, Glorieta, New Mexico, 1983 printing. Print.

Melody, Michael Edward, and Frank W. Porter. *The Apache*. New York: Chelsea House, 1989. Print.

Memorial and Affidavits Showing Outrages Perpetrated by the Apache Indians in the Territory of Arizona, for the Years 1869 and 1870. San Francisco: Francis & Valentine, 1871. Print.

Moody, Ralph. *The Old Trails West*. New York: T.Y. Crowell, 1963. Print.

Nelson, Richard K., and Terry P. Dickey. *The Athabaskans: People of the Boreal Forest*. Fairbanks, Alaska: U of Alaska Museum, 1983. Print.

Nelson, Richard K. *Make Prayers to the Raven: A Koyukon View of the Northern Forest*. Chicago: U of Chicago, 1983. Print.

Newton, Virginia. *The Carlota Project: An Ethnohistory Study etc...*, SWCA Inc, Environmental Consultants, Tucson, AZ. Archaeological Report #95-216, November 30, 1995. Print.

Officer, James E. *Hispanic Arizona, 1536-1856*. Tucson: U of Arizona, 1987. Print.

Olarte, Jose, and Elizabeth Ann Harper John. *Views from the Apache Frontier Report on the Northern Provinces of New Spain*. Norman, Okla.: U of Oklahoma, 1994. Print.

Opler, Morris Edward. *An Apache Life-Way...*, Lincoln. University of Nebraska Press. 1996. Print.

Ortiz, Alfonso. *Western Apache*: *Handbook of North American Indians: Southwest*, Vol. 10. Washington D.C. Smithsonian Institution. pp 462-488. 1983. Print.

Palmer, Edward. *Handwritten Notes from 1866*, Special Collections, Tuscon: University of Arizona Library. Print.

Pattie, James Ohio. *Personal Narrative of James O. Pattie*. Missoula, MT, Mountain Press Publishing Co, 1988. Print.

Phelps, John. *Beaver Trappers In Arizona History,* Wild Life Views, Arizona Game and Fish Department, April 1997. Print.

Pilles, Peter J. Jr. *A Review Of Yavapai Archaeology In The Protohistoric Period of the North American Southwest, AD 1450-1700,* edited by Wilcox and Masse, pp. 163-182. Tempe, AZ. Arizona State University Anthropological Research Papers, #24. 1981. Print.

Quebbeman, Frances. *Medicine in Territorial Arizona,* Phoenix, AZ. Arizona Historical Foundation, 1966. Print.

Redman, Charles L. *People of the Tonto Rim,* Washington, D.C.: Smithsonian Institution Press, 1993. Print.

Reed, Bill. *The Last Bugle Call*. Private printing. 1977. Print.

Rogers, M. J. "An Outline of Yuman Prehistory." *Southwestern Journal of Anthropology* 1(2) (1945): 167-198. Print.

Ruland-Thorne, Kate. *The Yavapai: Sedona's Native People*. Sedona, AZ. Thorne Enterprises Publishing Inc., 1993. Print.

Sacks, B. *Records Of Camp Verde, Arizona Territory*... typed from handwritten manuscript, copies in Arizona Historical Foundation, Tempe, Arizona; Arizona Historical Society Library, Tucson; Camp Verde State Park Museum, Camp Verde, Arizona. Date uncertain. Print.

Schroeder, Albert H. *A Study Of Yavapai History, Parts I-III*. Santa Fe, NM: National Park Service, nd.

Serven, James E. *The Gun - An Instrument Of Destiny In Arizona*, Arizoniana, Fall 1964, Arizona Pioneer's Historical Society, Tucson, 1964

Sherburne, John P., and Mary McDougall Gordon. *Through Indian Country to California: John P. Sherburne's Diary of the Whipple Expedition, 1853-1854*. Stanford, Calif.: Stanford UP, 1988. Print.

Schreier, Jim. *Hell Hath No Limits: The Army, the Apaches and Arizona's Camp Reno, 1867-1870*. Tucson: J. Schreier, 1989. Print.

Schreier, Jim. *Camp Reno: Outpost in Apachería, 1867-1870*. Tucson: Arizona Historical Society, 1992. Print.

Side Lights On Fifty Years Of Apache Warfare: 1836-1886. Arizoniana, Vol. II, #3. Tucson, AZ. Arizona Pioneer's Historical Society. Fall 1961. Print.

Smith, Jack. *A Guide to the Beale Wagon Road through Flagstaff, Arizona.* Flagstaff, Ariz.: Tales of the Beale Road Pub., 1984. Print.

Sparks, Joe P. *The Yavapai-Tonto Apache Indian Community at Payson, Arizona: A Position Paper.* Place of Publication Not Identified: [publisher Not Identified], 1972. Print.

Spicer, Edward Holland. *Cycles of Conquest: The Impact of Spain, Mexico, and the United States on the Indians of the Southwest, 1533-1960.* Tucson: U of Arizona, 1962. Print.

Stockel, H. Henrietta. *Women of the Apache Nation Voices of Truth.* Reno: U of Nevada, 1991. Print.

The Story of Pauline Weaver. (with Bruce Harper), np. Sierra Azul Productions. 1993. Print.

Stratton, R. B. *Captivity of the Oatman Girls.* Lincoln: U of Nebraska, 1983. Print.

Strickland, Rex. *The Birth and Death of a Legend - The Johnson Massacre of 1837.* Arizona and the West: Vol. 18, #3, 1976. Print.

Terrell, John Upton. *Apache Chronicle.* Thomas Crowell Co. 1974. Print.

Terrell, John Upton. *Estevanico the Black.* Los Angeles: Westernlore, 1968. Print.

The Territorial Governors of Arizona. Arizona Historical Review: January 1936. Print.
Tevis, James Henry. *Arizona in the '50's: The Memoirs of James H. Tevis.* Albuquerque: U of New Mexico, 1954. Print.

Thrapp, Dan L. *The Conquest of Apacheria*. Norman: U of Oklahoma, 1967. Print.

Udall, Stewart. *In Coronado's Footsteps*. Arizona Highways, April 1985. Print.

Underhill, Lonnie E. (ed.) *Edward Palmer's Experiences in Arizona*. Arizona and the West. Spring (1984). Print.

Underhill, Lonnie E. *A History of the First Arizona Volunteer Infantry, 1865-1866*. Unpublished, 1979. Print.

Utley, Robert M. *Frontier Regulars; the United States Army and the Indian, 1866-1891,*. New York: Macmillan, 1973. Print.

Utley, Robert M. *Frontiersmen in Blue: The United States Army and the Indian, 1848-1865*. New York: Macmillan, 1967. Print.

Wagoner, Jay J. *Arizona Territory: 1863-1912 : A Political History*. Tucson (Ariz.): U of Arizona, 1970. Print.

Wagoner, Jay J. *Early Arizona: Prehistory to Civil War*. Tucson: U of Arizona, 1975. Print.

Wells, Edmund W. *Argonaut Tales, Stories of the Gold Seekers and the Indian Scouts of Early Arizona,*. New York: Grafton, 1927. Print.

Wharfield, H. B. *Cooley: Army Scout, Arizona Pioneer, Wayside Host, Apache Friend*. El Cajon, Calif.: H.B. Wharfield, 1966. Print.

Whittlesey, Stephanie Michelle. *Vanishing River: Landscapes and Lives of the Lower Verde Valley : The Lower Verde Archaeological Project : Overview, Synthesis, and Conclusions*. Tucson, Ariz.: SRI, 1997. Print.

Williams, Eugene. *The Territorial Governors of Arizona*. Arizona Historical Review. July 1935. Print.

Wilson, David, and Arthur Woodward. "Benjamin David Wilson's Observations On Early Days In California And New Mexico." *Annual Publication of the Historical Society of Southern California*: 74-150. Print.

Woody, Clara. *The Woolsey Expeditions of 1864,*. Arizona and the West, Vol. IV, #2. Summer 1962. Print.

Worcester, Donald E. *The Apaches: Eagles of the Southwest*. Norman: U of Oklahoma, 1979. Print.

Photo Credits

Metates and North Peak	Stan Brown
Apache woman with water jug	Donn Morris
Gowas (Anna Mae Deming Collection)	NGCHS
Apache women and child	Postcard
Apache woman with burro	Unknown
Camp Apache, 1873	Public Domain
General George Crook	Public Domain
Troops before the Battle of Big Dry Wash, July 17, 1882	Public Domain
Indian scouts at Camp Verde, c. 1870	Public Domain
Guard house at San Carlos, 1880	Public Domain
Tonto Apache man, c. 1884	Public Domain
San Carlos trade token	NGCHS
Apache workers at Roosevelt, c. 1909	Public Domain
Henry Evans, Tonto Apache scout	NGCHS
King S. Woolsey	Public Domain
Apache crown dancers, 2014	Ann Baldwin
Apache burden basket	NGCHS
Apache beaded belt	NGCHS
Beaded necklace	Donna Daly
"Pitch Pot" (Rhea Delma-1950's)	NGCHS

INDEX

INDEX

www.ingramcontent.com/pod-product-compliance
Lightning Source LLC
Chambersburg PA
CBHW051819090426
42736CB00011B/1560

9780990356936